Scripture Led

Politics

... Mutual Exclusivity Be Damned

A. Dru Kristenev

Scripture Led Politics

Cover Photo: A. Dru Kristenev
First Edition ChangingWind: December 2012

A. Dru Kristenev

Psalm 22:28
For the kingdom is the Lord's: and he is the
governor among the nations.

Foreword

If the title offends you, then we're right on target. Our intent is to stir up a conversation that too many Americans have become uncomfortable discussing. Face it, we've been told so many times to avoid the two subjects of Religion and Politics that, frankly, we've forgotten how to address either one… at least with any sense or reason. Instead they have become taboo topics for dating, the dinner table, the water cooler (okay, make that the espresso machine) or anywhere else that citizens gather to work or play. Why? Because it *might* cause discord or impassioned disagreement.

Are we not civilized enough to be able to discuss, in an animated fashion, the facts of this world in which we live? If you listen to certain segments of our society, that is precisely the case. In fact, for each *side* just about every noun and verb employed in general speech have become "fightin' words." It seems to me that isn't such a bad thing. We must research in order to form educated opinions – something sorely lacking today – rather than assume that whoever is speaking, whom we may happen to respect, revere or even adulate, is infallible. The problem is that our education system has belittled critical thinking or redefined the term to mean acceptance of the professor's esteemed opinion as being, by way of his/her title, more worthy than ours. How many of us have fallen prey to that skewed thinking, whether it was a teacher, doctor, judge or pastor whom we simply wouldn't conceive of questioning their superior knowledge?

Speaking from post-graduate experience and years of teaching alongside many a Ph.D., allow me to clarify that the more education one has, the more indoctrination one has undergone. Whether that is to one's benefit or deficit, you may decide. Obviously, I have my own viewpoint.

Thus, I am here to present this forbidden twain of discussion topics, not singularly but as necessarily conjoined, in that we cannot understand societal mores, which influence legislation, if we have no comprehension of a foundation in faith… one does not mutually exclude the other. They must be entwined to provide a core for a social structure that works. Since we have been so jaded by the constant, and incorrect, citation of "separation of church and State" we have forgotten that religion, or faith actually, birthed this State.

What follows is a compilation of selected commentaries penned over the last four years with prayerful consideration that bring together, mix and cross-pollinate the truth of our nationhood: how the prohibited subjects of Religion and Politics are indelibly intertwined and must *again* become fare for thought… **and** daily application.

As Christians, it behooves us to remember that consistent study of the Bible opens new understanding at every turn, that our best intentions are hindered if we are unreasonably attached to our opinions. I thank the Lord each day for the privilege of having the opportunity to study with Godly, inspired and farsighted Bible teachers over the last decades who echoed Martin Luther when he entreated all to measure the truth of God's Word against God's Word: *"Sola Scriptura."*

A. Dru Kristenev
ChangingWind Ministry
ChangingWind.Org, Toddy Littman, Website Manager
December 3, 2012

Note: Apologies for those internet addresses that are no longer operable. As we all know, webpages come and go depending on (wouldn't you know it) political interests. The scrubbers are always busy.

Scripture Led Politics

A. Dru Kristenev

Table of Contents
Foreword
Part 1

Part 2

Part 3

Part 4

Epilogue

Part 1

Culture and Scripture

February 13, 2009
<u>The Golden Calf Revisited</u>

When we talk about history repeating itself we have a
tendency to think in terms of relative recent history, but in
this instance it would behoove us to go back a few millen-
nia.

Let's begin by pondering the free enterprise system
that has been the true stimulus of prosperity in this country
since its institution here by our forefathers. How, over
time, the hard work that each person expended could be
rewarded with wealth... a good life for themselves and
their families. It was all accomplished by following the
basic tenets of reaping what was sown through labor,
thoughtful investment and generous giving of the fruits of
that labor. Yet even as the benefits of diligent work were
heaped upon the populace, some among them were unhap-
py with working responsibly to create wealth for themselves. They grumbled that it wasn't easy enough to
become successful and they sought to have something,
some entity give them what they desired, even unto believing that that object was powerful enough to handle their
needs – feed them, clothe them, heal them. So they turned
to giving the foremost grumbler their assets so he could
manage them and borrow against them in order to fulfill
their wishes to be coddled, expecting a return beyond that
of the venture. Many expected to be included in the plan

even if they hadn't contributed.

But it was all an illusion. In fact, what was gathered was actually put into a bailout that only created more for those who controlled the bailout and they determined how, when and even *if* it was to be used. What the lead grumbler did was make a promise that the bailout would create prosperity simply by being established. That it wasn't even really necessary to actually distribute what had been gathered if a show of good intentions were demonstrated. And, all the while the people continued to believe that the almighty bailout was being made for them, to help them, to provide jobs and allay want.

This is no different from the Israelites who, having wandered only a few months after being freed from captivity, grew weary of what had already been provided for them. They were fed morning and night, given water and asked only to follow the rules of personal responsibility in order to reap true freedom and contentment, which lay just beyond the horizon. While Moses went onto the mount to receive instruction on how this multitude could truly flourish, they grew restless. Less than forty days did it take for them to turn from the good life they had been provided to proceeding to pile all their gold into the crucible to fashion, not a miraculous bailout, but a miraculous idol. It was a golden calf that would answer all their desires, not because it had any real power or even was able to give a moving speech to assure them of happiness and wealth. No, it was because they simply wanted to believe that it could cure all their ills, real and imagined. And this they did after they had already experienced the benefit of following the guidance of the Lord to reach a true goal.

They abandoned what was real in favor of an empty promise.

Tell me how this is not precisely what has swept

through our country now? How is it that a tried and true method of hard work and responsible action embodied within the free enterprise system can be tossed aside when an arguably charismatic character comes forward and promises "change" that will give them "more"? Have we so lost our way in the wilderness that we will gather up our riches, hand them over to a man and a Congress who will create another golden calf for us to fawn over and worship because it will magically provide what we think we lack? If you listened to the questions directed at President Obama during the town hall at Ft. Meyers, Florida on February 10, 2009, you would certainly think that is the case.

We are blinded by the manipulation of a limited number of power brokers who have facilitated the creation of an economic "emergency." Hm-hmmm, right. This is such an emergency that the first idol, in the form of TARP, didn't do its job and wasn't even fully utilized. And now we are urged, panicked rather, to believe that the bigger and better golden calf will cure our ailments when all we need do is allow the proven market to step in and naturally guide us back to fiscal health over time.

No one said it would be an easy or simple road. Not even God told the Israelites that they'd reach their goal without a little sacrifice and some work. No, He laid out a method by which the multitude could improve their lot, but they preferred a quick fix, an unproven "hope" – basically, a fantasy. A fantasy that rewarded their foolishness with forty more years of unnecessary wandering.

You show me how the power of a golden calf is no more imaginary than that of the so-called stimulus package.

A. Dru Kristenev

✣ ✣ ✣

December 3, 2009 – *And we just voted in more of the same...*

October 17, 2009
<u>Humanity Under Siege</u>

If you thought that America was the land of the free. You're right. It was.

No longer.

With every passing day, Congress and the Administration are working to keep you busy with personal struggles to put food on the table and gas in your car while they further their battle against you. Yes, I said *against* your interests. If you think I've gone around the bend here are some things to consider before you write off the concept with a flick of your hand.

As soon as Mr. Obama took office the onslaught began in earnest. With each passing week, multiple new bills were shoved through by the Democrat controlled Congress. We were suffocated with stultifying debt: American Recovery and Reinvestment Act; Omnibus Appropriations Bill; Obama's New Era of Responsibility $3.5 Trillion Budget. We were shown to the queue for compelled volunteer work and inviting terrorists to come live among us on *our* dollar: Generations Invigorating Volunteerism and Education Act. We were given untenable regulations for energy production and consumption: American Clean Energy and Security Act of 2009 passed by the House.

Now we are further threatened with executive power to disrupt any and all internet communication: CyberSecurity Act of 2009; and the incursion expands in scope to overtake all of our health care decisions, including first taxing us for three years without benefit and then dictating how we use our hard-earned dollars to pay for it: America's Healthy Future Act (Baucus Bill) http://www.cnsnews.com/news/article/55425 and America's Affordable Health Choices Act of 2009 (House version).

The problem is, if we thought that this is everything that is in store for us, we are sadly mistaken. The battle against not only Americans, but humanity in general, has been ongoing for decades. Virtually every "beneficial" bill enacted by Congress from the Clean Air Act and Clean Water Act to innumerable lesser known legislation, which was voted in under the good intentions of keeping our environment livable, have actually ushered in regulatory forces that make our world unlivable. We have been delivered into the hands of those who know better than us how we should make our living, feed our families and care for ourselves, even down to being directed on how our exhalations are murdering the planet and it's bounty.

I have no beef with protecting the environment from destruction. However, the scientific research upon which these ordinances and laws are enacted must be factual, not the trumped up cries of Chicken Little disseminated to strike fear into the hearts of children, children who then panic that it is their duty to save an earth over which they have no power. Even to assume that humanity can utterly destroy the planet is beyond arrogant. We can't even agree on how old is this earth, let alone how long it will last.

Our science is educated (and often not so) conjecture. Every day, scientists discover new facts about the universe, macro and micro, that changes their suppositions regarding the attributes of physics, even unto questioning what were earlier presumed to be "laws" thereof.

No. No man has the intuitive or intellectual power to

know what is inherently good for the earth, nor does he/she have the insight to proclaim what is good and proper for each individual's life. There are those who would usurp all decisions unto themselves regarding our well being, placing us, each human who would presume to make a decision about their lives and livelihood, under siege.,, a siege of burdensome taxation and legislation that will ultimately destroy us.

It makes one wonder when ultra-environmentalists have plainly stated their premise that humanity is nothing more than a virus upon the pristine planet. What does that make every other organism that has thrived on the earth? Certainly no more valuable to the system. You can't have it both ways. If you believe that all living things came about randomly, then all living things have an equal beginning and an equal rationale to exist and all living livings thus classify as virus, i.e. pestilence.

Personally, I have more respect for God's creation. What about you?

A. Dru Kristenev

✤ ✤ ✤

June 23, 2010
Discourage best friends? Who's idea is that?

Why on earth would teachers and school administrators meddle in the natural affinity of children and youth to develop special friendships? For teachers like me, who don't follow the "group-think" mind-set that is forwarded among curricula for educators today, the concept is absurd.

The idea of dissuading children from forming close friendships on an individual basis, http://www.nytimes.com/2010/06/17/fashion/17BFF.html, seems more akin to social engineering than creating a healthier social network.

Discouraging single friendships and pressing for "pack" socialization, creates mob mentality, pure and simple. When a group of kids (or adults) operates as a unit, there is less individual responsibility for actions, instead a mob atmosphere can develop. This is when people get hurt and is the root of bullying, a problem that has reached almost epidemic proportions to the point that all levels of government are now legislating against it, and schools are forming committees to fight the growing phenomenon. "Socializing in a pack" is counter-intuitive. It limits intimacy and increases the probability of criticism, and even condemnation, rather than creating an atmosphere of giving and caring.

Isolating individuals by driving them to "herd" devalues individual thought and growth, directing people toward a victim attitude and, ultimately, the solace of government in tough times. And now, we are witnessing the most destructive of mob behavior. No longer are flash mobs benign, but now we are seeing "flash robs."

The thinking that these social engineering educators have birthed is the concept that being among "friends" it matters not what these youngsters do, or that they take the time to evaluate their actions. Accountability has fled to where even anti-social behavior is tolerable, including teens, communicating via social networks, swamping businesses with the intent of stealing goods and destroying the storefront. Looting by "twitter."

This is not all. It also portends the destruction of the Church by discouraging people from forming close friendships, prayer partners, small worship groups, quaint quilting bees, anything where moral, like-thinking people gather to share and comfort one another. Instead, the idea of kids playing at the park by appointment, or roving in insensate packs at a mall, promotes the easier acceptance of modern cultural mores that override the family as a guide for life values. It engenders peer pressure activity, another bullying tactic.

Individual friendships could be likened to a threat to the State. Even the early Church suffered from dividers who told members that they shouldn't think alike, shouldn't believe alike, be in agreement. Gnosticism sowed dissent by infiltrating the young congregations touting that common "knowledge" was superior to faith, and forming friendships in the faith, that the shared beliefs (a basis for best friendship) was detrimental to personal development. Consider this... how best for a governmental institution to maintain control if not by encouraging formation of large groups that establish "suitable" expectations for members, induce irresponsible behavior, and discourage intimacy? Intimate friendships allow for free sharing of ideas and experiences, large groups may not because they invalidate critical thinking, creating a breeding ground for censure.

This is what many educators are trying to do today. First, they are well trained in class management, not the skillful teaching of subject matter. Secondly, the dissolution of the institutions of faith, which is the foundation of our unique government, creates an environment that undermines the patterns of life for everyone; stripping them of individual thought and sharing by providing them with "group-think." Heard that before? But it wasn't so far off the mark when Orwell, an avowed socialist, coined the term in "1984." Can't have best friends if it endangers the growth of collective thinking, an action which undermines the message of love, light, and faith that is the core of Christianity, can we.

The idea of socializing without special bonding or a moral base is the harbinger of bigger and "badder" things, like social groups that formed the basis for the unthinkable, unthinking organizations like the Hitler Youth, which definitely wasn't the Boy Scouts. "Flash robs" are just the beginning of this trend toward cruelty.

No, "best friends" are a danger to the growth of government oversight by giving kids a chance to air their most intimate thoughts and feelings with another child, believing that the sanctity of friendship will most likely not be betrayed. Yes, infidelity and duplicity can occur among children and youth in building friendships, but at least they learn the valuable lessons of loyalty that come with the territory. Social packs don't allow for the development of individual thought and trustworthiness, they encourage the need to "fit in," to conform. And where is there room for honest expression in a State where differing opinion can't be tolerated?

A. Dru Kristenev

September 10, 2011

Just a few interesting things to consider on Acts 5...

*5:3 – When Peter asks Ananias "why hath Satan filled thine heart to lie to the Holy Ghost?" he expands on that in 5:4 – "why hast thou **conceived** this thing in thine heart?"*

Satan is the "adversary" and the "accuser" according to Strong's and the Greek is synonymous with the "devil" (traducer). God notes man's penchant for being His adver - sary from the beginning (Gen. 8:21 "...for the imagination of man's heart is evil from his youth.") and the conception of evil, what Peter tells Ananias he has done (conceived) the evil in his heart, it indicates man's ability to create evil thoughts within himself, and assuming the role of adver - sary. Mark 7:21-23 "...out of the heart of men, proceed evil thoughts..."

Peter also in 5:9 asks Sapphira "how is it that ye have agreed together to tempt the Spirit of the Lord?" bringing up the fact that one cannot tempt (test) the Lord, Matthew 4:7, as the Israelites did at Massah (Deuteronomy 6:16, Exodus 17:2-7), which is what, in Ananias' and Sapphira's hearts, they were attempting (tempt), by even "conceiving" that they could lie to God.

What it proved was that they had not given their hearts to Christ in the first place, and were still tied to the world, and thus, satan, which is of the world, in that they didn't (couldn't) understand how the giving worked and believed it better to "attempt" (tempt) to hide things from the Lord. Only one who is deceived, or deceives himself, thinks to "tempt" God.

My mention of the story in Acts was written in response to a Progressive's claim that collectivism is a scriptural tenet:

March 27, 2011
<u>Early Church Collectivism?</u>

Perhaps it's a sign of the times, or secular education, that there would arise a discussion as to how the fledgling church promoted collectivist ideals. Stretching scripture to unwieldy bounds, some overly analytical minds have posited that a singular point in the New Testament illustrates a legal Marxist-Pharisaic correlation. Having spent far too many years in the hallowed halls of university, studying and teaching, it was no surprise to come across the determination to prove worldly mores among the spiritual Word.

I take you to the story of Ananias and Sapphira, from which this hypothesis was derived. Within the discussion did I hear no reference to any other biblical cite. The first rule of Bible study is to test scripture against scripture, the concept which fired Martin Luther to post his 95 Theses on the doors of Castle Church in Wittenberg, Germany that sparked the Reformation. In this, nothing has changed. Scripture must be tested by scripture.

Setting that premise aside to comply with the conversationalists' basis for conclusion, the Book of Acts is opened to Chapter 5. For ease of the reader, I will use both KJV and NIV translations. http://www.biblegateway.com/passage/?search=Acts+5&version=KJV
http://www.biblegateway.com/passage/?search=Acts+5&version=NIV
Beginning in Verse 1, the couple has sold their property in preparation to give part of the proceeds to the young church under the guidance of Peter. However, they withhold some of the money, lying about the amount they received when Ananias makes an offering. Being caught

by his own deceit, he is struck dead. Unknowing of her husband's passing, Sapphira also speaks with Peter and following her husband's example, she also lies about the money received, nor does she escape the same death sentence.

Some contributors to the discussion seemed to claim that the reason for the pair's demise is directly related to the law, that which the Pharisees interpreted and enforced among the Jewish population. Although this scripture deals with the newly risen church, their assumption is that the legalism of Judaic tradition formed the basis for the church rather than faith in Christ's resurrection. First mistake.

Secondly, these seem to also assume that possessions were subject to collection for the temple to be redistributed among the priests, lawyers (Pharisees), scribes, Sadducees and people. Another mistake. Tithing is firmly established in the Old Testament, as well as specifics for types and amounts of livestock or harvest to be burnt offerings, all in relation to the sin to be expiated, or thanksgiving to be acknowledged. Yet not all of one's goods were to be given to the upkeep of the temple, Cohanim (priestly class), the king, or even the collections for the needy. There was no regulation barring private property, as the Communist Manifesto dictates (Section II. Proletarians and Communists: "...In this sense, the theory of the Communists may be summed up in the single sentence: Abolition of private property.")

The standard for offering is first set by Abel, Gen 4:4-7, that the best of the best was to be given to God, "firstlings of the flock and of the fat thereof. And the Lord had respect unto Abel and his offering." The establishment of the worthiness of the sacrifice is all throughout the Book of Leviticus, Lev 1:3; Lev 3:1; Lev 2:1; etc. And let us not forget the remonstrance of Solomon in Proverbs

3:9, "Honor the Lord with thy substance, and with the firstfruits of all thine increase." Remember Jesus overturning the tables of moneychangers and dove sellers in the temple? Did he not do so because offerings were no longer presented prayerfully as the best of one's labor, but purchased at will, signifying a lack of forethought and true sacrifice, having become a trade and an affront to God, Matthew 21:12?

The last misunderstanding in this discussion regarding Ananias' offering is in not recognizing that all sacrifice, as offered within the temple, was no longer necessary. Offerings on the altar served as the shadow for the ultimate sacrifice made by Christ on the cross. Once that final sacrifice of the Holy Lamb, Jesus Christ, had been made, the law for all believers, was written on their hearts, Jeremiah 31:33, utterly fulfilled, and could not be satisfied through worldly actions and literal execution of the law, Hebrews 10:14-18.

So why did followers of Christ such as Ananias and Sapphira even give to the Church? It was not a requirement to discipleship, not in the fashion of institutional giving to the temple, or even a collectivist concept (which did not exist in pharisaic tradition). The reason for giving is rooted in Christ's message of love – charity is the all-encompassing term used in the KJV – and gratitude. There is no purpose to make an offering to God if it is not given with a thankful heart, the crux of acceptance for Abel's and every gift thereafter set before the altar in the Old Testament, and into the hands of the New Testament Church.

Why these two people gave up the ghost upon their dishonesty has to do with acceptable offering, or a willing gift. Peter is clear when he tells Ananias that he had power to do whatever he liked with his property. The apparent intention of Ananias was to hide his wealth and to give without a pure heart, not that keeping back some of his earning was disallowed by law or Christ. This is what Peter called to his attention, that the worldly view of wealth eclipsed his own readiness to give freely and gratefully. Fear of relinquishing what was his (the young ruler, Mark 10:17-25, Luke 18:18-25), or control of his circumstances, caused him to attempt to hold back truth from God. The inability to walk in faith, and to think that he could hide his heart from God, was Ananias' undoing ("I know that thou canst do every thing, and that no thought can be withholden from thee." Job 42:2).

The acceptable, respected offering is that which is given freely, with an open and thankful heart, whether it is part, or in some cases, all of what one has (the widow's mite, Luke 21:1-5). It is the spirit with which it is given, not the amount. We are even told to bear our own burden, to take pleasure in creating with our hands, providing for ourselves, Galatians 6:4-5. Howbeit then, were one to give all that they own to the Church (or the State, in Marxist terms), thus becoming beholden to others' ability, or inability, to provide for the now penurious person, would they be better off? As each of us are provided gifts and talents to use to the benefit of others and ourselves, does God demand that we divest ourselves of those tools, those gifts, in exchange for dependence on the generosity of society or a hierarchy? This is the Marxist model: to give up our livelihood to be given a living, i.e. welfare.

The church model is to offer the best of our gifts, our increase, to our brethren knowing that we are further blessed by giving, being able to offer more as we endeavor more to create a livelihood. All in right standing with God, spiritually directed in our hearts to share what we can, and sometimes, even what we cannot afford.

The concept of giving all that you own to follow Christ is thus a spiritual offering, having no relationship to the Marxist ideal of everyone contributing all their worldly wealth into one pot, that a ruling elite would then distribute according to your need and their so-called wisdom.

Christ *is* wisdom and when the believer walks in faith, delivering his life to God's hands, he is blessed with peace, knowing that he is giving how and when directed by the Spirit, not hiding from the Holy Spirit, as was Ananias.

A. Dru Kristenev

✠ ✠ ✠

May 10, 2011
Elijah's Fellow Disciples

During this most recent ministry walk of the last eight months, the Lord has been faithful to supply every need.

Reaching a point where the nation's financial drought became ever more evident, I was shown to leave a place of repose where all necessities were covered, during which time certain work had come to completion. As Elijah had hidden by the Brook of Cherith, fed by ravens and watered by the stream until it dried up (1Kings 17:1-9), the message came that it was time to go... someone had need in another place. And here have I been for a time, offering what little blessing the Lord has placed at my disposal to share.

It was here, deep in prayer in this last place of refuge, that the story began to unfold, somewhat akin to the tale of Elijah. Grappling with the growing acceptance of false perceptions pervading our nation, (environmentalism, communism, the deceit of "democracy," and government dispensation of rights to the people) there has been a growing need to, not only tell truth, but call out to all citizens to discard erroneous teachings about the founding of this country, and the direction wherein lies salvation.

False prophets run rampant, invading every aspect of our society – schools, entertainment, government, family and fellowship, and even the church – with errant "knowledge" – much as Israel was under the thumb of Ahab's wife, Jezebel, her prophets bowing and sacrificing to Baal, encouraging and causing the people to turn their back on God.

It was at the apex of this backsliding that Elijah was

brought out of hiding after three years of drought, to oppose Baalim with a test of the sacrifice (1Kings 18). When Elijah's sacrifice was consumed by holy fire, after Baal's prophets' offering had been ignored by the lifeless idol, he was called by God to slay all those false prophets. Upon all 450 of them being slain by the hand of Elijah, he informed Ahab that the drought was ended (1Kings 18:41). Yet Jezebel uttered a threat to Elijah and he fled to God's holy peak, Horeb, Mt. Sinai, crying to God, thinking himself the last one in the struggle against idolatry. Here, the Lord told him that there were yet seven thousand left who had not bowed their knee to Baal (1Kings 19:18), who were yet faithful to God. Elijah was not alone.

As Elijah was obedient to God's word, slaying the false prophets with the sword (the scriptural embodiment of the word of God – Ephesians 6:17), we answer the call to slay the false prophets of our time with words, that righteous sword supported by the Word. And as Elijah was not the only one of God's disciples left, we also are among the thousands, even millions, who have not forsaken the truth to follow after deception.

It is within our power, as sovereigns by God's blessing, to return America to its right standing with God by acknowledging our Christ-driven roots, and endeavor to re- establish that essence of our nation.

Elijah's tale is a beacon for us to follow, slaying the deceivers with the sword… and the sword we wield are words… words of truth that can and will recapture the heart of America.

A. Dru Kristenev

✛ ✛ ✛

June 11, 2011
Empathizing with the homeless

Have you ever really wondered what it would be like to have no address, no front door to unlock, or bed on which to lay your head at the end of day? Most of us don't, though we like to think that we can truly empathize with the individuals who are actually in the face of real-life homelessness. And I am not talking about those who have managed to drop to the depths of society by surrendering their lives to addiction, or simple sloth.

These last nine months have been an eye-opening experience as I, like many other under-employed professionals and laborers, have seen a dramatic change in circumstances. My own journey has been one of ministry. A journey that the Lord took two years to prepare me to undertake, because I fought the idea of leaving for parts unknown until the choice had been made for me... not enough work to sustain myself, and furthering of the mission placed on my heart to serve.

Why is this story being told? To bring it home (pardon the pun) that there are hundreds of thousands of productive individuals in this country who have been forced to throw in the towel. The difference between many of us is that some refuse to go on the government dole. No matter how bad the situation, some individuals will stand their ground and go to the source of charity (that means 'love' for those who don't crack open their Bible now and again), which is the church. By this, I mean God and His family, the body of Christ, the believers, not some imposing building straddling a city corner, occupying prime real estate.

In fact, it takes far more fortitude and courage to place

your faith in God and fellow believers than a corruption-laced bureaucracy led by corrupt power-mongers who heartily subscribe to the idea they are your betters… the politburo that directs the proletariat, crushing workers until they become virtual serfs, wholly dependent on the policy-makers.

Did I say that it takes courage to run the economic gauntlet without becoming a ward of the state, subservient, and relinquishing dignity in exchange for a government check? With good reason is this point made, because it is with fear that anyone marches into the uncertain future, beset with the knowledge that they have no clue where they will find work or, sometimes, even their next meal. Christ said it in such a way that we cannot bypass his meaning when he told his disciples in Matthew 6:25-27. "Therefore I say to you, do not worry about your life, what you will eat or what you will drink; nor about your body, what you will put on. Is not life more than food and the body more than clothing? Look at the birds of the air, for they neither sow nor reap nor gather into barns; yet your heavenly Father feeds them. Are you not of more value than they?..." NKJV

Or how simply Paul put it in Philippians 4:6-7. "Be anxious for nothing, but in everything by prayer and sup-plication, with thanksgiving, let your requests be made known to God; and the peace of God, which surpasses all understanding, will guard your hearts and minds through Christ Jesus." NKJV

Since when can you lift up your prayers to Father Government and receive peace in knowing that you have value in its eyes? In fact, by receiving more and more from government, one actually denies their value as an individual, accepting that they are to be swept hither and yon, wherever and whenever some human decides they are worthy of notice, and hence, giving a pittance for their pocket – which likely has holes, half the amount being reabsorbed by the very government that tapped the public till in the first place.

God sees value in all He creates… you and me, and it is His will to guide each of us to a better life, one of inward peace, were we to trust Him to do so. It is by God's Grace, received by Jesus' sacrifice, that we can look home-lessness in the face and not panic, however much we may want to do exactly that. "Fear not" is the recurring theme throughout God's word, and it is earthly fear that drives us to reach for the handout offered by government drabs rather than, if we listen, knowing where to go to see fulfill-ment of God's promise to us. No, it is not a matter of wishing on a star for food or clothing. It is up to us to hear how we should set forth, one step at a time, to reach our goals of providing for ourselves, and, when we have arrived at that abundance, turn around and share with oth-ers following. Many of us have lived the cycles of abun-dance and want. "I know what it is to be in need, and I know what it is to have plenty. I have learned the secret of being content in any and every situation, whether well fed or hungry, whether living in plenty or in want. I can do all this through Him who gives me strength." Philippians 4:12-13 NIV.

It's not an easy journey, as one who is mid-trail (you could also read that as mid-trial) is finding out. We are all in transit. It is our choice to be one who gives, and in hard times has the graciousness to humbly receive. It is our duty to follow our hearts in so doing rather than to mind-lessly sign over earnings to government pimps working without accountability or conscience.

The question is… what are we going to do about it?
The choice is ours.

A. Dru Kristenev

July 19, 2011
Empathy Part 2...
<u>Are we being fed or feeding fear?</u>

We've all heard or made reference to the Good Samaritan, though we may not know the whole story, only that the title refers to such a person who will stop and help an individual unknown to them, in their time of need. Isn't this an attitude to which we all aspire? To be someone who'd stop to assist another after an accident or some misfortune? Most likely, you're bobbing your head that you would do so, or even recalling a time when you did just that, dropping what you were doing and running to help someone in a dire situation.

Or have you?

In this day and age, too many of us are either too busy, or too frightened, to undertake the burden of helping another, be it a large or small thing. And we certainly might not think to ask someone if they required help. Do you know why that is? You guessed it. I have a couple of theories extracted from years of observation and experience, and perhaps even a little study.

We've become so inured to the tragedy that pervades our world, whether depicted through media or occurring a block from home. Shootings, stabbings, drug-induced violence, natural disasters, automobile accidents. There is an unending inventory of bad behavior and unfortunate circumstances that unfold all around us, fully covered by media hounds eager to show the vile underbelly of society. And it is done with barely concealed glee, validating the official line that society has reached an irreversible point of destructive conduct, redeemable only by authoritative

A. Dru Krístenev

intervention, i.e. government, or for others, God. The Good Samaritan is rarely found because people fear being slapped with a lawsuit for "interfering" with authorities. Or… being drawn into a situation that impedes their lives, or, even worse, places them in danger, is a constant worry. Perhaps they will pray for divine intervention.

Many may not realize that this tale of the Good Samaritan is a parable Jesus told to a lawyer, a Pharisee, whom He guided to answer his own query, regarding the attainment of eternal life, by condensing the Law into this statement: "Thou shalt love the Lord thy God with all thy heart, and with all thy soul, and with all thy strength, and with all thy mind; and thy neighbour as thyself." Luke 10:25-27 KJV. This naturally led to the next question of, "…and who is my neighbour?" Luke 10:29.

The story tells us how two upstanding, religious members of the community, a priest and a Levite, minded their own business when they spied a man, one of their own, broken, beaten and robbed, lying in their way. It was too much trouble for them to turn aside from their own priorities to help an unfortunate man who had been assaulted and left to die. (Did you think that this was a new phenomenon of modern society? Hardly.) Jesus didn't say whether they prayed for the man. Not much later came a passerby, a Samaritan, who bore no goodwill for Jews, yet he halted in his journey to assist the victim of crime. Not only did he bind the man's wounds and set him upon his own mount, but he took him to an inn and charged the innkeeper to take care of the man, paying the proprietor a good wage and promising, upon his return, to cover all costs incurred (Luke 10:30-37).

Whoa, he did all that for a stranger? And for one whom, under other circumstances, he might even despise? Hard to believe for 2000 years ago, let alone in this day and age. Evidently, man hasn't really progressed all that much, if at all. Of course, today, we would dump the victim on the Department of Social and Health Services, let them become a ward of the state while we went on our unencumbered way, maybe praising our selfless action. Some might even add prayers for his recovery. The problem is believing that this is preferable to personal involvement. What it truly is, is dehumanizing.

Have you figured out what Jesus was saying yet? That everyone is our neighbor, not just the fellow who parks his SUV next door, with whom we probably haven't even exchanged names. If we are to "Do to others as you would have them do to you," Luke 6:31 NIV, then why would we reflexively call social services instead of reaching out ourselves? The plain answer is the same now as it was for the priest and Levite… self-interest and fear.

What is fascinating in this story of the Samaritan is that it coincides with the fact that some Christians today are less apt to act than unbelievers, just as the Samaritan, an unbeliever, was the one to shoulder responsibility and help a stranger.

Fear enters into the equation when we see the evangelical, so beset with worry over the coming end, that they are overwhelmed with preparing for times of tribulation, unable to see past their needs of stocking up. Then, there are other believers, expectant of impending doom, who have abandoned the love walk in favor of simply waiting and watching in despondence as the world spirals toward destruction. Fear has infected our Christian mores of loving our neighbors as ourselves. While we study end times and pack away provisions, we often ignore the needs around us, abdicating our responsibility and leaving inefficient, taxpayer-funded government agencies to take up the slack.

Then, there is pride. Pride in our years of study of scripture drives us to keep a tenacious grip on viewpoints that can blind us to the grace under which we thrive. So sure of ourselves that we are interpreting the Word with accuracy, that fear of the future, which is meant to free us, becomes a new form of bondage. A reinstatement of the legalism that gave rise to the behavior exhibited by the proper priest and Levite in Jesus' parable.

Where are our priorities as believers? Doing what's undemanding has become habit (which can include the most heartfelt prayer) and the Samaritan, the unbeliever, has been the one who has often been moved to do what's right. It is a shameful dilemma we face as Christians, unable to look beyond our own comforts and personal needs (our "box" embodied by religious passivity and tunnel vision) to help in a tangible way, not just dig into our pocket and hand over a few bucks. That's too easy, and an excuse not to fulfill God's direction, because anything more may be troublesome, an impediment to our lives. Indeed, we must watch after our own, but we are bound by our faith to be ready instruments of relief when we are able, not just when it is convenient. This is our testimony. Prayer is the communication line with God by which He informs us of how we *can* do what is possible for us *to* do, not just to wish for a miracle from Heaven.

Perhaps that is the problem. Our lives of convenience, instant gratification, and unwillingness to step outside our comfort zone, have left us devoid of empathy for others' trials, only able to focus on our own. The NIMBY mentality has tainted the Church.

Decisions are to be made founded in faith and constant prayer (1Thessalonians 5:17), rather than fear. We are exhorted to do no less. Yet, we must be receptive to how God answers our prayers, because it may be through us that He acts.

Let me ask this… whose test is it when we find ourselves confronted with someone's need where we may be instrumental, as earthly angels (messengers), in our ability to help? The person in need? Or us, challenged to do what's right?

A. Dru Kristenev
"Empathy, Part 2…" is the follow-up to
"Empathizing with the Homeless," June 10, 2011

✤ ✤ ✤

September 10, 2011

This was written a couple of months ago, yet it seems more relevant now with the constant flood of falsehoods from the office of the President, the media and members of Congress regarding this debt ceiling "crisis." Toddy Littman has written on this issue from so many angles dis-pensing the truth that if, by now, you still haven't received the message that we are under attack by lie after lie, then you need to go back to our website, ChangingWind.org, *and read in more depth. With fact in our hip pocket we can take our place as disciples of the truth and redeem this nation...*

Empathy Part 3
How do we give in tough times?

"For if there is first a willing mind, *it is* accepted according to what one has, *and* not according to what he does not have. "[13]For *I do* not *mean* that others should be eased and you burdened; [14]but by an equality, *that* now at this time your abundance *may supply* their lack, that their abundance also may *supply* your lack—that there may be equality. [15]As it is written, *"He who gathered much had nothing left over, and he who gathered little had no lack."(Exodus 16:18)* 2Corinthians 8:12-15 NKJV

Fear of not having enough is encountered at every turn, whether in a metropolis the size of New York, a manufacturing town in Germany, or an impoverished village in Uganda. As much as the media has touted the end of the recession, too many are feeling the effects of what could be called a depression. Homes are going back into the hands of the bank – do you recall the Great Depression tales of unemployed workers and businessmen losing their

homes to foreclosure? – factories are closing doors, send-
ing jobs overseas or just folding for good; the cost of gro-
ceries and fuel are spiraling out of sight so the soccer mom
can't afford to pay to travel to work, let alone ferry the
kids to practice; retail outlets disappear as blocks of empty
storefronts take their place.

We aren't so naïve as to believe that the world's economy hasn't taken a nosedive. Everyone is feeling the
effects, and governments are breaking under the weight of
social programs and union coercion. The second wave of
rioting in Greece, protesting necessary government austeri-
ty measures (6/15/11), the rioting in Britain starting August
6, 2011, and the longshoremen's union in Washington state
(9/8/11), using pressure tactics and violence trying to force
funding of their pension plan,
http://online.wsj.com/article/SB100014240531119048361045765569 7
1275750328.html
exemplifies the growing crisis, and the unconscionable
expectation of entitlement.

On top of which, we feel that our hands are tied to do
anything useful, our own resources being tapped out, or
nearly so. It is in times such as these that our Christian
mores should stand forth, an example of light in a darkling
world of hunger and homelessness. But are we making that
stand? Too many of us are chagrined at our own lack of
selflessness, and we know that we are not doing what we
could.

Look to the widow's two mites (Mark 12:41-44) as she
gave what she could ill afford, when the temple powerbro-
kers dropped in their contribution of what they could easily dispose. Here does the teaching of Paul follow the point
made by Jesus who watched these proceedings occur. The
willingness to offer what we can muster carries so much
more weight than depositing an amount that means little to
us, or thinking government should dispense aid in our

stead. If our action in helping others has no impact on our lives, if it is nothing more than an idle donation, given by rote (or taxes), then we gain nothing from the exercise.

The equality to which Paul refers us, is that of heart to give, not the amount or the ability to do so. Abundance comes in surges, the swell of much often cycles with the outgoing tide of lack. We are either swimming in plenty, dry with little, or, most often, wading through just enough to get by.

Wherever each of us finds ourselves in this economy – struggling through the current, or comfortably floating on the surface – we are taught to take responsible action toward our neighbors, be it a little or a lot. The attempted regulating of individual wealth (or lack thereof according to government statistics) destroys the compassion of sharing, and on the opposite side, the humility of receiving.

The Church, meaning the individuals who make up the body, the corpus, shows us that material goods distract us from what is of true value… fellowship with Christ and one another. This is the core of giving: fellowship, because in this do we experience completion. By relying on government to oversee social redistribution (rather like re-gifting in the bureaucratic world), which was just reiterated Thursday when the President urged the Congress to pass yet another debilitating spending bill, we lose contact with our Creator, and ultimately ourselves. Communication breaks down and society deteriorates. Just look at the violence erupting around the globe as those who literally fight to receive what they believe their due, have lost common ground with their neighbors, remaking them into adversaries who "owe" them.

Christ taught us well to have our hands out to help, and when we must extend that same hand to receive, we ascribe true value to what is offered.

A. Dru Kristenev

Scripture Led Politics

✤ ✤ ✤

November 5, 2011
<u>Obama Administration: No recognition of God</u>

One can only find it disturbing that the Obama Administration always appears to be on the side of refusing to acknowledge God whenever an opportunity to do so arises. Even in this instance where the republicans are essentially acting to honor a democrat president, after whom Obama has gone out of his way to pattern himself, by adding the D-Day prayer of Franklin Delano Roosevelt to the WWII Memorial in Washington, D.C.

http://www.foxnews.com/politics/2011/11/04/obama-administration-opposes-fdr-prayer-at-wwii-memorial/

Personally, I thought God is God, by most standards whether you are Christian, Jewish or even Muslim, but this outward rejection of any mention of God makes me wonder at Obama and his administration's definition of the Almighty. Particularly as Obama has repeatedly vocalized his adherence to Christianity, this objection to FDR's supplication for God's "blessing we shall prevail over the unholy forces of our enemy," presents reason to question his declarations.

While the president of the Family Research Council calls this stance anti-Christian, it is most alarming in regard to the thought that perhaps there are those in the Obama employ (including the president himself), proclaiming admiration for Islam, who evidently don't equate Allah with God. And this, after we have been told repeatedly that Allah is another name for God.

So, which is it? My guess is (and I'm sure this will raise the ire of every liberal and Muslim who hears of it) that faith in Allah and our faith in God *are not the same*

thing. Why else would Obama and his acolytes disclaim God at every turn? Note how he slams Speaker Boehner for stating our motto as being, "In God We Trust."

http://www.foxnews.com/on-air/hannity/index.html#/v/1257325676001/is-there-a-solution-for-americas-economic-crisis/?playlist_id=86924

My answer is simply that Obama and his entourage accept the fact that this is a nation built by Providence, God's hand (no Allah here) in the establishment of this unique form of government that, for all liberal assertion of the United States being a democracy, absolutely is not. Let a strong suggestion be made herein that they actually read our true history, as opposed to the revised progressive version circulating in public school textbooks. Perhaps then, the words of our founders would resonate, for in God we ***do*** trust.

A. Dru Kristenev

✥ ✥ ✥

June 22, 2012
Founding principles never included progressive tax:
**How can we, individually and as a nation, continue
to help others if we are robbed of the means to do so?**

The needs of so many are met by Americans through
thousands of hope missions at home and around the world.
They are missions both faith-based and secular that are
supported wholly by individuals giving from their personal
fortune, large or small. Ask yourself this, how will we be
able to continue to finance the altruistic work done in our
backyard and internationally if we are robbed of that
increase by government grasping, the invasive hand of
government growing government (power) that helps no
one *but government*?

This is the case *against* progressive income tax and *for*
individual freedom to give from the heart.

Let's get down to the nitty-gritty right at the start: A
progressive income tax is the government adopting the
idea that when some people reach a certain level of
income, it is assumed they are then taking from others,
increasing poverty by creating wealth. It presupposes that
most individuals aren't smart enough to make their own
way, despite what the President said today at the NALEO
conference about people coming to America for that
express purpose. In fact, the erroneous idea is that there is
a finite amount of wealth and if someone makes a lot of
money it automatically confiscates that potential income
from someone else, creating a poor underclass. Now, if
this isn't plain folly, if not moronic reasoning, than I don't
know what is.

What *is* true, is that when government establishes a

progressive tax in order to steal from the rich to give to the poor (the Robin Hood idea which we'll discuss further on in this article) **no one** is served. The government, which is no longer representing you and me but itself and self-per-petuation, has instead collected income that goes nowhere but into self-directed projects promoting the creation of "victims of society," i.e. welfare addicts.

Back to the beginning of this country and the Framers' intent, the change of former servants to become masters, and realize that now the reverse has occurred where the elected servants have usurped the role of master. Note that it was the government that amended the Constitution to gather income tax, not the People. The purpose of the 1913 beginning of this boondoggle was to collect money to fund projects and entitlements that were _never_ designated under the Constitution.

Article 1, Section 8: *Congress having the power to tax, etc. "to pay the Debts and provide for the common Defence and general Welfare of the United States."* As Toddy has expounded upon numerous times, http://changing-wind.org/index/comment.php?comment.news.185, http://changing-wind.org/index/comment.php?comment.news.151, this is the defi-nition of "welfare" used within the context of the United States Constitution (note the designation specific to states):

Welfare: Noah Webster's 1828 Dictionary:

2. Exemption from any unusual evil or calamity; the enjoyment of peace and prosperity, or the ordinary bless - ings of society and civil government; applied to states.

Thus were (and are) taxes never to be collected for the purposes of providing education, promoting arts or even providing for the poor, the "welfare" programs, i.e. entitle-ment programs. Read Jefferson's second inaugural address (fifth paragraph) in the first article link above.

As to the point about government amending the

Constitution as opposed to the People's endeavor, after the 14th amendment was ratified, all amendments to the Constitution were undertaken by government *for* government and not at the behest of the People as this was the composition of the Congress... it no longer was a representative body but had transformed itself into an authoritative, i.e. ruling, body using the victory over the South, and now subordinate States, in order to introduce the alteration of intent and implementation of central governance.

The Reconstruction Acts were enacted as a means of subjecting the vanquished States to regulations imposed by the winning faction, passing racially motivated (divisive) legislation and regulations, such as tax laws that promote racial and economic separation among the people and fostering a growing polarity between "classes" that would fuel the infusion of communistic ideals: democracy. Already, the 1848 manifesto of Karl Marx and Friedrich Engels had finagled its way into the matrix of America. (Check "The Call" to form the first teachers' union in 1857. http://changingwind.org/index/comment.php?comment.news.148)

Now, to get to the redistribution and divisiveness of the progressive tax we can add the "noble" persona of Robin Hood, whose compassion for the deprived and downtrodden drove him to appropriate from the rich to "give" to the poor. Not exactly a Christian message, when it comes right down to it. Wherein is it a noble thing to raid a man's storehouse in order to care for the poor? In this case there is no generosity, just envy, thievery and deceit. Throughout Scripture we are encouraged to care for the fatherless, the orphans and the widows. Nowhere are we told to take from someone else in order to do so.

So we come to the Robin Hood Tax, which world leaders, philanthropists and unions are promoting as a righteous act. In May, Lou Dobbs gave a rundown on the pro-

posed international FTT, Financial Transaction Tax, and the overlordship it would create should the sanctimonious have their way – for we know that only they, the wealthy liberal elite, understand the needs of the poor and under-privileged and how best to serve them.
http://video.foxbusiness.com/v/1646570386001/un-unions-push-for-robin-hood-tax/

That day, nurses representing the NNU (National Nurses United) were dancing in the streets at the NATO conference in Chicago in support of a Robin Hood Tax. http://foxvalleylabornews.com/2012/05/25/nurses-rally-in-chicago-calls-for-robin-hood-tax/. All of this pomposity has led to a crying for a new homegrown version of the FTT with minor celebrities and a few leftist economists, just this week, beginning their own promotion of **taxing financial transactions to underwrite their own "good-for-every-body" agendas.** http://www.csmonitor.com/USA/Politics/The-Vote

Luckily, it's going nowhere in the EU as even the Irish finance minister "…noted that this is the first time enhanced cooperation would be used on a major economic dossier "setting a precedent over taxation, a sovereign mat-ter."" http://euobserver.com/18/116732

Something we must remember at all costs: the move-ment to encroach on United States sovereignty, specifically the People's sovereignty, comes not only by way of a push to instill an international taxing authority, but the wholly unconstitutional inflicting of the progressive tax as it exists now. And the so-called Robin Hood Tax is just another way to implement a progressive tax on the "undeserving" rich.

To clarify, our purpose here is to inform and arm you to jealously defend the freedoms recognized and guarded by our brilliantly crafted founding documents. Because, only by standing with our country's framers in their desire to provide for our free creation of wealth will we be able to continue providing freely for the welfare (in the first definition of Noah Webster pertaining to individuals) of suffering people the world over, and following the Lord's instructions for true charity… the expression of love for our neighbor.

Thank you for reading,

A. Dru Kristenev and Toddy Littman

✠ ✠ ✠

August 12, 2012
Obama's Alternative Energy Cabal

Although the word 'cabal' came into common use after the early 1600s, the Chaldean root: *to acquire*, fits right in with the more modern definition of a conspiracy or plot, as in overthrowing a government. Why else create a 'cabal' if not to acquire power?

You must be wondering why I've chosen this particular word to describe what President Obama is about when he already occupies the most powerful office in the land, and as generally accepted, the world. This is going to be a deep discussion, so hang onto your scuba mask so you don't drown under the obfuscating rhetoric and blow-by that continues to spring from the oval office.

How many of us have truly considered who are the beneficiaries of all the 'green' bucks that continue to be laundered through the executive branch? The multiple billions of dollars that have been awarded via Stimulus and grants constructed to prop up the alternative energy industry – a term used for lack of a better one since there is no actual industry in motion, just a scheme (look up that word, too, while you've got your dictionary handy) – are going precisely where?

In answer to that, there is the oft-mentioned $535 million to Solyndra, but let me add these few to the list:

• $186 million for federal weatherization in California produced a total of 538 full-time jobs; 3 homes weatherized and 14 jobs in $20 Million grant to Seattle

• $510 million in stimulus loans and grants to green-tech companies: Tesla Motors, RecycleBank, EdeniQ and Amyris. http://www.forbes.com/sites/larrybell/2011/09/06/president-

obamas-green-jobs-pretense-is-an-unmitigated-fiasco/. And then
there's the Soros' investments in 'green' tech growth capital with government funds http://changingwind.org/index/com-
ment.php?comment.news.167
(though you'll be interested to know that both articles
linked therein are, strangely, no longer available...
hmmm).

Although these are drops in the bucket, as they say, it
should be noted how hedge funds that drive oil speculation
and oil moneymen like T. Boone Pickens are now hip-deep
in 'green' technology. Why is that? And why are think
tanks like the Milken Institute pushing for federal
Competitive Renewable Energy Zones to tap into the $11
billion for grid upgrades 'created' by the American
Recovery & Reinvestment Act of 2009. By the way, isn't
Milken, better known as the junk-bond king, the guy who
went away for securities fraud? We should examine where
our advice originates.
http://www.renewableenergyfocus.com/view/8419/designate-renew-
able-energy-zones-across-us-suggests-think-tank/ What is most disturbing is the assumption that government can and should
design and implement the "plan" for grid modernization to
accommodate government-driven (read that "compelled")
private investment into "renewable" sources that maybe
pans out to 20% of (unreliable) energy generation, with
losses of 40% in transmission alone over copper conduc-
tion lines. (Kristenev, A. Dru (2009). *Energy Barons*.
ChangingWind, softcover edition, Page 418)

Who, then, is Obama, our ultimate **corporate (billionaire) lobbyist-in-chief for alternative energy**, as Toddy
tags him, working to benefit? Certainly not the average citizen, you or me, as we will be in hock to the handful of
billionaires that own the rights to this or that technology
that "converts" the wind, Sun and whatever other inconsis-

tent and obscure energy source they can conjure up for "usage fees." President Obama is the frontman for the legal regime that *manufactured the separation of mineral rights from those of the land*, thereby dividing property owners from the full usage and enjoyment of their land. And what about airspace? How does that figure in to this creation "of a legal system to control invented energy generated by inventions?" (I stole that from Toddy Littman, too.)

Think about it. Harnessing contrived methods of transmitting free energy, the only purpose of which is to take profits... who can afford the manipulation of government and the political hacks in order to accomplish this except for the small number of outlandishly wealthy such as the Soros' and Buffetts of this world? A scheme is built where a contraption like a specialty windmill "gathers" energy <u>without burning, or really "generating" anything</u>, as opposed to what occurs with coal, natural gas and oil, all to sell to the highest bidder, who then backs the socialist government which gets its cut via leases. The cycle is self-proliferating... lawyers breed laws that feed the money-source that engenders the governmental regulations to keep the circular-dwindling of individual rights in motion. **The entire thing is owned by the invention owner because the legal regime was created for that purpose, to bilk the people through the legal control of the alternative energy industry, being defined by government as a "public utility" and given a specific local monopoly.** Beyond that is the fact that there is no liability to the invention owner. Do not forget that most <u>legislation quite often is created to protect government, and its cronies, from liability</u> (which is the whole point of lobbyists like Obama).

This all goes to the "*end user* license agreement"

applied to every use of technology, including now the "generation of energy." Here again we will be "licensed" to use energy. The more we license, the less we own, because we relinquish our rights in favor of government-granted privilege, "government-granted" because it is a privilege created by "legislation," known to the "end user" as a license. This is the road to capitulate to government, "constituted" by us to be our servant, handing over to government the free usage of our property in exchange for an "allowed" use (so long as we pay the government fee of course), wherein it is a "use crime" to access it unless duly licensed.

We shall go one step further. Recall the June 28, 2012 ruling of the Supreme Court (note our last article: "Let's go back to Egypt; Freedom is just too hard") to understand that **the Obamacare decision opens the door for a government mandate to purchase energy according to government standards.** The days of culling energy with a personally owned windmill, solar panels or even a wood-burning stove could be over. Instead, you'd be taxed, or fined for "generating" your own power except under government purview and by prescribed acceptable means. Even the gas station will go by the wayside, replaced by a "power station." Funny how all that stimulus money that was designated for electric vehicle charging bases that never materialized, seemed to dissipate into thin air. The Phoenix company, eTec (parent company ECOtality) secured a $99.8 million stimulus grant in 2009 (part of the $2.9 billion to DOE) to build 12,000 charging stations across five states http://www.usatoday.com/news/nation/2009-11-03-electric-cars_N.htm. They have released almost nothing to the press since August 2010 http://www.etecevs.com/pdf/08242010_Biden.pdf. So, where have they been and what have they done with all that cash?

Looks like they're using part of it to sue California energy regulators for giving a contract to build charging stations to NRG, a New Jersey outfit.
http://articles.latimes.com/2012/may/26/business/la-fi-nrg-charging-20120526

Oh yes, it looks like they've built 556 of the planned 12,000 plug-in corners thus far
http://www.blinknetwork.com/locator.html. That's progress as progressives look at it. On top of that is the ridiculous cost of the electric vehicles in the first place, not to mention that those charging stations are still being powered by coal. (Charleston Daily Mail, 12/14/10: "National energy policy isn't making much sense; electric vehicles depend on coal; wind and solar can't supplant it")

We are witnessing cronyism at its worst: Obama working the country as lobbyist-in-chief to corner the alternative energy market for his billionaire chums, trying to persuade his constituency that he's a "man of the people" when, in truth, he is anything but. He *is* a sellout and corporate toady. He's also the one who said we want to be Brazil's (Petrobras) "biggest customer" for oil, the company that saw Soros' investment of U.S. funding not once, but twice (Progressive Brute Force Marketing: Egypt). Obama is setting up for the oil barons to become the *alternative energy barons*, plain and simple.

Who loses? You, me and all the minorities Obama calls his base, who are facing bankruptcy at the hands of White House crony energy policy. New energy scheme, same owners, same old cabal, yet with greater financial leverages, no cost of drilling, no cost of mining. It's all in who owns the "rights to harness" the movement of the oceans, or the wind, where maintenance is the highest "cost of production," irrespective of the intrinsic environment over our own land being made unavailable to us for our use without paying The Alternative Energy Piper Lord their homage, what they so appropriately call "royalty" á la "end user license fees."

Thank you for reading,

A. Dru Kristenev and Toddy Littman

✛ ✛ ✛

November 12, 2012
Hierarchy of Freedom

How do we, individually and as a nation, define free-dom? There has developed a great divide in America regarding this fundamental concept. Approximately half of Americans who vote seem to think that freedom is receiving benefits from the government when the exact opposite occurs under this misguided notion.

Living within the borders of the United States has bred an isolated vision of the rest of the world. Many Americans have created a bubble around their lives, assuming that their actions inside their homes and work-place have no consequences regarding, not only their immediate neighbors but, others around the globe. This is nothing new to humanity. We have always been accus-tomed to seeing after our own needs and, frankly, given to ignoring those of others, believing that someone else will take up the cause. In fact, this is the core of the problem when it comes to the government collection plate.

The reference to the church is intentional to illustrate the correlation, as opposed to the struggle, between reli-gion and State. Plainly, the idea that each person should contribute to the overall care of others is universal. What it has spawned in an increasingly Godless world, is the expression of government as a god, the attempted replace-ment of God by non-representative bureaucracy, where even the elected, supposedly advocate officials take a back seat (it's called 'delegation'). Thus taxes (tribute, rather, when you take the concept back to its origin in the world of kings and despots) become the collection plate, they are the tithe to the new "church."

Freedom comes from a place completely divorced

from the State, however this is no longer understood due the populace having been "educated" to "know" that spiritual connection to God does not exist, that only self has purpose, and self is ultimately egocentric, and thus blind to others' needs and consequently inefficient in serving those needs.

Think about it. How can a person, who only subscribes to the paramount fulfillment of their own want, be able to recognize the need of another, let alone truly care about helping them? This is the rationale behind bureaucracy, agency and political manipulation of government. It is impersonal and operates for agency self-perpetuation before all else. Need proof? Just look to the ineffectual relief efforts for victims of super-storm Sandy and recall what *did* work in Joplin, Missouri after the tornado and Nashville, Tennessee after the devastating floods – individuals, churches and private organizations successfully undertaking the rebuilding.

This is the difference between Spirit and society. One is connected to hearing conscience to direct personal action and the other is "being" conscience for those "less fortunate," and dictating process. The first is accountability and the second is irresponsibility.

So how do we become responsible? First and foremost, by paying attention and laying aside emotionalism in favor of action. Seventy percent of Americans state that they are Christian, yet we do not act like it, disallowing Spirit to guide everyday decisions, and actually sloughing off decisions to others. This is the concept of paying into a big pot that someone else will distribute as they see fit. Yet when the distribution is overseen by those lacking conscience (political and social agencies), no one is served, not the giver nor the intended receiver. And iniquity flourishes. Yes, I meant what I wrote, though some may think that "inequity" is what I should mean, however that implies that certain people know how to create a just world. We do not. Only God understands the needs of all and is able to move our hearts, through His spirit, to respond to those needs. And this freedom in Christ, allowing ourselves to be moved by the Lord to abandon self-absorption to do what is right to serve, rather than be used by other societal entities, is the liberty sought by those who first arrived on these shores and who have come later.

Individual freedom comes from reliance on God, not a State (humanity's idea of equity or justice). It is the understanding that His spirit will guide us to do what is right in our own homes, among our family, our friends, our neighbors and as the circle expands, in treating strangers. Nothing can replace God. Not another person and certainly not a State agency that has no conscience. In America, we have been given the freedom to act according to God's will. The ego of about half of those who voted, however, have used the corruptible system – as are all man's systems – to restrain that freedom; relieving individuals of their personal liberty over their thoughts, their honor, their posterity and their wealth.

If America is to survive (and, in all truth, I entertain doubts that it will), we must re-establish our connection to God and restrain the grasping growth and evolution of the State into something it was never intended. It means that we need to understand the difference between the Law of the Land that is the Written Constitution, and the periodic statutes that come and go, such as the Affordable Care Act. Only then will we restore our ability to give and help others in ways that are efficient, purposeful and with a thankful heart.

Can those who believe the fallacy of State benevolence be convinced of truth? Questionable, but that should not defeat the effort to teach truth and, once again, direct our efforts to reclaim the freedom of individuals in this nation to garner wealth that provides the true freedom to give as God guides us… the freedom to serve. (Deuteronomy 15:10-11)

A. Dru Kristenev

✚ ✚ ✚

December 14, 2012
God, man and guns

If you're thinking that the recent spate of gun violence pervading the newscasts at Christmastime has anything to do with the inherent evil of firearms, you need to pay attention. Though, if I were a bettin' person, I'd lay money that you'll be the first to ignore what comes next and assume there's nothing new to be learned. Your mind is made up. Well and good, but you're missing out on information that you likely won't hear anywhere else... it isn't P.C.

This morning, a young man walked into a Connecticut elementary school and opened fire on precious children and their teachers after apparently having murdered his own mother in her bed. As the story is still unfolding and the victims are reeling from the shock and heartbreak, some of these facts may be corrected as new information is divulged from the crime scene, yet it changes nothing regarding the heinous act and the cause of it.

I speak not specifically of the perpetrator's mindset. I have no way of knowing what that was other than assuming that he was somehow mentally or emotionally disturbed, but it changes not one iota of the cause, and that was of his own making.

Last night, I received an e-mail from a fellow missionary who shares scripturally-based meditations each day and his question was, which lie do we believe about God... that He is not who He says He is, or that we do not believe who He says we are? A question with far more depth than most realize, and one that has relevance to the vicious acts we've witnessed just this last week alone. As a Christian, one is exhorted to not only believe God but place faith in what He says regarding Himself, that He is the author of good, (Genesis 1; Exodus 34:5-7) and what He says of us in that we are His children and transformed by Christ whom we carry in our hearts.

Is this confusing to you? Let me explain as best I can, being a simple ambassador of Christ, not a scholar; but then, the message of Christ is actually quite simple.

The general secular belief is that man is innately good and it is society that leads the individual astray. Of course, were that the case then society would never have the opportunity to misguide the individual because society is, from the outset, an invention of man, and if man is good then society would reflect that in its influence. In fact, the exact opposite is true, and, unfortunately, born out at every turn of which today's incident is a tragic example. Scripturally speaking, man's heart ("mind" or "thoughts" in the Old Testament Hebrew sense) is "evil from his youth." Genesis 8:21, also Genesis 6:5. Basically, man is self-centered and his thoughts, if left to himself, revolve around himself... that's "me, me, me" to you. Proverbs 22:15 tells us, "Foolishness is bound in the heart of a child; but the rod of correction shall drive it far from him." And God is that disciplinarian, so "Trust in the Lord with all thine heart; and lean not unto thine own understanding" - Proverbs 3:5. Plainly, man's understanding is flawed.

As details continue to be revealed about the tragedy that occurred in Newtown, Connecticut where the shooter is being described as "troubled," it is essential that we put the terminology in perspective: the more we, man, rely on our imperfect judgment, our emotion-driven thoughts, we are apt to act foolishly and, in this case, with cruel and evil intent. It was not guns that perpetrated this deed, nor was it God, but a person who acted according to his own skewed thoughts, expectations and feelings. Man has been given freewill that all too many employ it to their shame, then improperly lay blame at the feet of God when they alone must bear the guilt. It is not a matter of God "allowing" these crimes against the innocent, it is a matter of man operating on his own volition, without a connection to God.

The simplicity of the message to which I referred? Once we place our faith in God we are able see the greater picture, taking our focus off of ourselves and our self-indulgent character. God's plan completes man's make-up in answer to man's imperfect understanding and egoism, and that plan is the acceptance of Christ within his heart, Romans 12:2 . The enactment of more of man's faulty ideas and societal regulations will not change his heart or influence his natural bent. Only the gift of grace through Christ's sacrifice can accomplish that. When man accepts the gift, his heart and mind is turned and the unthinkable indeed becomes the unthinkable and, as such, is never committed.

Man can't fix himself, try as he might through therapy, peer counseling or legislation. Guns are only tools utilized by an individual to good or evil end. God is not the source of the individual's decision to act fiendishly, but He is the saving grace for one to turn aside from evil.

A. Dru Kristenev

✠ ✠ ✠

Part 2

Repeating History

March 19, 2010
On the edge of the wilderness... again
    (Healthcare – A Mythical Pony Ride)

Here we stand, perched at the precipice, the brink of the abyss, and not for the first time.

History tells us that we have been at this same cliff time and time again. It also tells us that we have willingly jumped without looking either forward into the future or, most importantly, behind us at our past folly. To this end, this morning I was struck with the realization that I have been driven twice in this last year to write about the correlations between our country's choices and those of the Israelites wandering in the wilderness.

http://changingwind.org/index/news.php?extend.51.6
http://changingwind.org/index/news.php?item.64.1

I don't believe that it was to no purpose, even if I was speaking to no one but myself, which is likely the case this time as well. Even so, I will take us down that road one more time. Don't they say, "third time's the charm?"

We were led out of slavery more than two hundred years ago by men who heeded destiny, in the words of George Washington and others, Providence, a divine guide. We have since tried every sidetrack possible to lead ourselves back to slavery, just as the Israelites did. Even after their deliverance into the Promised Land, every forty years in fact, they managed to turn aside from truth and right to worship at the feet of idols. Each time they faltered, they petitioned God for rescue and He pulled their fat out of the fire.

Why can't we see that every scheme this administration is plunking down in front of our avaricious eyes is nothing more than an idol, an empty promise? Why do we insist on believing in some supernatural fix from Washington when we have the power to follow the right path, to take responsibility for our idleness and sloth? Sure, I'm using harsh words, but doesn't our distraction from our representatives' actions in the capital by only attending to our everyday needs (and wants) amount to laziness? We have delivered our government "by the people" to a charismatic figure and his followers who "do *to* the people." We shut our ears to truth and allow the silken lies to soothe us while we're stripped of everything for which our forerunners fought and died.

There is no prophet in the White House, unless you believe in the change that the occupant promises, the "transformation" of our country. I don't know about you, but I differ with the man sitting in the Oval Office, this country is not in need of transformation other than our putting the bridle back on this government and reining it in.

Sweep the idol off the altar and close down the health care myth, because that's all it is... a phantasmagorical ride on Pegasus' back.

Take those reins and pull hard.

A. Dru Kristenev

✟ ✟ ✟

November 28, 2011...

Although this was written months ago, the timing for it seems to be upon us as the Occupy Wall Street groups have taken to burdening society with their destructive/obstruc - tive behavior, spreading violence and pestilence, and dis - ruption of orderly life of those who are productive, simply to sow discontent and harbor unethical behavior. These are the actions of "entitled" individuals (70+% of the demonstrators are trust fund babies) raised without a moral compass or any notion of personal responsibility, all of which is addressed below...

May 13, 2011
<u>Anarchy – Not Chaos, but God as King</u>

God had His plan from the beginning.

The line of communication first established with Man was delivered by the "Breath of Life," (Genesis 2:7), 'neshamah,' that God transferred into Adam, establishing the unique connection. This is spirit through which we, as God's creation, conversed with our Creator. He reigned absolute and we came directly to Him with our thoughts and concerns.

And then, the trust was destroyed by Man's shunning of God's decree in his wish to be like God and to know the difference between good and evil, the one thing from which the omnipotent and omniscient King protected His children, His creation and charge.

The connection between God and Man was severed... until God's plan to re-establish that bond would come to fruition. Yet, throughout the travails of man over millen-nia, God gave him opportunity to repair the rift, time and time again, opportunities that man squandered. There were few who heard God in the antediluvian age, so few that God finally destroyed man except for one servant who listened, Noah, with whom God confirmed his promise, as a rainbow spanning the sky, to spare the world the same calamity in the future (Genesis 9:11-14).

Still, faith was a little known commodity among creation populating the earth. From thence until Abram, did God find few willing to listen, follow, and serve Him with their whole heart (Genesis 12:1-4). Through Abraham came the seed that God would bless, and bring forth progeny with whom He would establish communion. Always, these particular people had a line of communication, a way of making supplication to the King – God – who ruled directly over the people covenanted with Him by circumcision (Genesis 17:10). No other people had this special reign of God directly over their lives. Other peoples of the earth relied on human kings and princes to wield intercessory power over them in the name of idols, their false, impotent gods.

All through the sojourn in Egypt, even when Israel was subject to a mortal monarch as slaves, did they continue to give spiritual fealty (sacrifice) to God alone, separating themselves from the polytheistic nations governed by earthly sovereigns. Even so, the coming of Moses to free them from physical and spiritual bondage was not readily accepted by the million souls he led forth from Goshen, they having become accustomed to Pharaoh's dominion. As creatures of habit, their inability to accept God's sovereignty, proven through 40 years of miraculous occurrences from which, incredibly, they rebelled, led that generation to be lost in the wilderness, never to lay eyes on the Promised Land.

God had given the Israelites the option to follow Him

alone, His presence always among them, first as a Pillar of Fire and Cloud (Exodus 14), then in the tabernacle housing the Ark of the Covenant. Moses was the mouthpiece, the holy appointed magistrate, for their sovereign Lord in whom they were to place all faith, a government administered by God through the holy priesthood... the test of faith that they so miserably failed.

Joshua sustained the theocracy after crossing the Jordan, receiving the figurative staff of Moses to lead Israel to the Promised Land (Deuteronomy 31:23). There, God resided with them, rescuing and judging from the mercy seat of the Ark of the Covenant, leading the Israelites in battle, blessing them in peace. The generational cycle of doubt and falling away from the Lord's direction to embrace idolatry, only to be saved by prayerful supplication of God's chosen judges, continued.

The sequence was ever-repeated as the Levitical anointed consistently fell away into the depths of iniquity, until the day Israel cried to God to become like the other nations of the earth. They were willing to discard God's perfect and sovereign rule to become subject to another fault-filled human (1Samuel 8:4-6). They rejected the perfect for the incomplete, weak and flawed, wherein God told them exactly what wickedness and betrayal they would suffer through that denial of God's perfect nature (1Samuel 8:7-18). How is it we still wonder at the adage warning us to be wary of what we ask because we know not the consequences of our foolishness?

The perfect rule of God from His earthly throne upon the Ark was the embodiment of a true anarchical society. Anarchy has changed in its definition to be regarded as inciting chaos when, in fact, if individuals inherently respect the rights of others, society comes as close to utopian as possible. In this we pay attention to Judges

21:25 "In those days there was no king in Israel: every man did that which was right in his own eyes." The rule of God is a rule of the heart and requires the internal acceptance of God's precepts, giving rise to good judgment when dealing with other individuals. Christ put it plainly, "So in everything, do to others what you would have them do to you" Matthew 7:12 NIV, which we universally call the Golden Rule.

God placed himself on the throne in the beginning and for all time. It was in consideration of this holy sovereignty that our founding fathers drew up the documents by which this nation was conceived and implemented… the recognition of the spirit of Christ, the Holy Spirit, within believers that connects man directly to the Father, giving rise to respect others' rights as equal to their own. Once man had rejected the rule of His true King when they came to the Prophet Samuel asking for a worldly ruler, there was no way to come home again until Christ came to bridge the spiritual gap, to fill the void. At which point, we are said to share with Christ his inheritance as he "…made us kings and priests unto God and his father," Revelation 1:6 KJV; "and hast made us unto our God kings and priests; and we shall reign on the earth." Revelation 5:10 KJV

Christ having come to bring the message of God's kingdom, even then did the Jews expect the establishment of a physical kingdom, urging Jesus to take an earthly crown, "When Jesus therefore perceived that they would come and take him by force, to make him a king…" John 6:15 KJV, he repudiated the concept of becoming a 'head of state,' knowing that the kingdom which he had come to establish was one of faith, invisible to all but those who understood with their hearts. Jesus clarified his place in a spiritual kingdom when rebuking the adversary, Luke 4:6-8, "…for it is written, Thou shalt worship the Lord thy

God, and him only shalt thou serve." Governance on earth is to glorify God as the only master.

Isaiah, in the first chapter, also brings dominion full circle for God's people, words which can be applied to this day and age, where he foretells the turning away of the faithful. Once the "dross" is purged, God instructed... "And I will restore thy judges as at the first, and thy counsellors as at the beginning: afterward thou shalt be called, The city of righteousness, the faithful city," Isaiah 1:26 KJV. This very concept stands behind the Declaration of Independence, where unalienable rights are affirmed to be God-given and we are all endowed as sovereigns under God's authority.

This domain would be utopia, the anarchy that despises the elevation of one man above another in governance, reserving that exalted reign for God alone... God who is delivered to us through the resurrection of His Son, Christ Jesus, who is the incarnation of Justice delivered by Love... God's love for his wayward creation, Man.

A. Dru Kristenev

✢ ✢ ✢

October 16, 2011
New Rise of Gnosticism – Heresy of the First Church
Revisited

This is not the first time I have referred to Gnosticism regarding the "transforming" of our nation into something unrecognizable to our Founders, as well as those of us growing up understanding that our rights are "endowed by our Creator." The heresy encountered by the early church was fully described by Irenaeus, the martyred Bishop of Lyons, in his tracts from the second century A.D., "Against the Heresies." Irenaeus was just one generation removed from the Apostle John and his teachings, the truth of grace and mercy still solidly standing at the core of the fledgling Church. He had full understanding of the movement to inculcate worldly, fallible "knowledge" within the Christian church as the central tenet rather than belief and faith in Christ's sacrifice to secure salvation for Mankind.

It is not without careful consideration that I used the words "Secular Gnosticism" in the article penned the day after the 2008 election
http://changingwind.org/index/comment.php?comment.news.27 or find myself right back at the heresy of Gnosticism, and by indirect association, humanism, as the root of our country's demonstrated demise under the leadership of President Obama.

Although we don't often hear reference to the "pleroma" or other equally absurd concept in Gnostic general usage, it is evident that the philosophy has infiltrated our Judeo-Christian ethos. Just look how the related language that arose in the Griswold v. Connecticut decision…
"…penumbras, formed by emanations…" http://www.law.cor-

A. Dru Kristenev

is right out of the Gnostic handbook. If you actually
thought that these terms were in reference to science, take
another look. In Gnosticism, emanations are from the universal spirit (pleroma - the spiritual universe that birthed a
pantheon of entities under the overall title of god) to the
world. Basically, the shadow of some universal "spiritual"
voodoo has been absorbed by our legal system (and the
subsequent flood of legislation undermining freedom by
regulation) to give credibility to a purely vile concept. This
is the incursion of immorality into a nation based on
Christian morals, no matter how much non-believers wail
the opposite to be true.

Take a look at what one of the finest Catholic theolo-
gians of the last century, Hans Urs von Balthasar, had to
say:

*"In the Middle Ages, from the Calabrian monastery of
Fiore, the doctrine of Abbot Joachim was to exert an
incalculable influence on later generations which has last -
ed to the present day. He thought the age of the
Incarnation of the Second Person of the Blessed Trinity
(together with the organized structure of His Church)
would eventually 'dissolve' into an age of Pure (Holy!)
Spirit. This spirit – passing through the stages of the
Renaissance, the Enlightenment (Lessing), Idealism, and
Marxism – degenerated into the purely human spirit of
atheism."* Urs von Balthasar, Hans (1981). Translated by John
Saward (1990) *The Scandal of the Incarnation: Irenaeus Against the
Heresies* (pp. 4-5). San Francisco. Ignatius Press.

The Gnosticism of Irenaeus' age is at the heart of modern atheism that has infiltrated our society with dead ideals
that lay the foundation for serfdom, the belief that there

are others of higher intellect who should, no, **must** wield power over the uninitiated fools who follow faith.

The panacea is not embodied by the renamed aristocracy of communism, which leadership in Washington has attempted to emplace. In actuality, it *is* faith in God. The faith and understanding as plainly stated in our Declaration of Independence that secures our rights, "Governments are instituted among men, deriving their just powers from the **consent** of the governed..." not the other way around.

Gnosticism is the worship of "knowledge" in its quest for the unknowable, which leads to adulation of petty deities that come under a plethora of new names from 'Science' to 'Gaia' in our modern world, and some other little known inventions such as 'emanations' that are ascribed intermediary power in creation. In the past, and still, these intermediaries sported names like Demiurgos, Aeons, etc., and they relegated Christ to one of these nondescript mini-deities.

What is most amazing about Gnosticism (and the eastern philosophies) that the "enlightened" espouse, is that their ideas are encumbered with an unending array of gods and goddesses, innumerable "ages" instigated by some "divine" action of odd deities, made up of multiple godheads and personalities, all of which are impossible to follow, or to know, which is a base belief of Gnosticism, that the "true god" is unknowable. In fact, Gnostics state that their philosophy must be explained by way of myths in order to be grasped. And this is what is supposed to be more comprehensible than the simple Christian understanding of one perfect Man taking on the sins of the world, past and future, as the embodiment of all sacrifice, by His suffering on the cross, once, for all. God, who, in contradiction to Gnostic thought, *is* knowable through the Holy Spirit, which resides in the hearts of the faithful.

Those of us who have opened our eyes and ears to understand the completion of the works of Christ, realize the simplicity of God's grace and mercy... that it isn't encumbered by hundreds and even thousands of petty entities that take on individual characteristics of what is all-encompassed by God. Talk about making life complicated. In fact, the humanist view, which those who propound it say, *"Humanism is a philosophy of reason and science in the pursuit of knowledge. Therefore, when it comes to the question of the most valid means for acquiring knowledge of the world, Humanists reject arbitrary faith, authority, revelation, and altered states of consciousness."*

Yet, the next statement is... ?

"Humanism is a philosophy of imagination. Humanists recognize that intuitive feelings, hunches, speculation, flashes of inspiration, emotion, altered states of conscious - ness, and even religious experience, while not valid means to acquire knowledge, remain useful sources of ideas that can lead us to new ways of looking at the world. These ideas, after they have been assessed rationally for their usefulness, can then be put to work, often as alternative approaches for solving problems." http://www.americanhumanist.org/who_we_are/about_humanism/What_is_Humanism That is precisely what the believers in "pure" science (random life) and worldly wisdom (corporeal senses) expect "smart" people to accept – a contradiction.

Listen to Irenaeus in *"Against the Heresies"*...

"This idea [that subordinate beings were responsible for the material world] may well entice and seduce those who know nothing of God and imagine Him to be like needy human beings; they, after all, are incapable of mak - ing anything immediately and without assistance, but need

all manner of instruments to produce what they want..."

Men who must try to understand the "unknowable" through what they know (intellect) are thinking backward. God, the omnipresent, who was before and is after all things, omniscient and omnipotent, is not based on His creation. This is what modern science calls anthropomorphism, an utterly narcissistic viewpoint of the universe that does not exist. Isaiah 45:18-19 is clear, and simple...
"**18**For thus saith the LORD that created the heavens; God himself that formed the earth and made it; he hath established it, he created it not in vain, he formed it to be inhabited: I am the LORD; and there is none else. **19**I have not spoken in secret, in a dark place of the earth: I said not unto the seed of Jacob, Seek ye me in vain: I the LORD speak righteousness, I declare things that are right."

When I passed a billboard asserting the notion, "think before you believe," it became quite evident that nonbelievers in God and Christ should turn the concept back upon themselves as they advocate the most complex knot of beliefs that compose faith out of faithlessness. Americanhumanist.org obviously espouses conviction in things unseen and, to all intents and purposes, nonsensical and nonsensible. It is almost amusing, were it not so tragic, that the champions of accumulating knowledge in all its forms assert beliefs that are far more convoluted than accepting the straightforward fulfillment of God's promise of grace.

As one woman I admire, who responds to the irresponsible ideas assigned to Christian faith by non-Christians through her e-ministry, queried in answer to the billboard's message of "think before you believe"... she said, "Yes, why don't you."

A. Dru Kristenev

A. Dru Krístenev

✛ ✛ ✛

December 11, 2011
<u>Repeating history... again</u>

It is perplexing that we, as a nation, are so willing to follow leaders claiming to have the truth in their palms without making the slightest effort to back-check, fact-check or apply the commonest of sense. This is obviously not man's first rodeo, though it may be yours.

Our predecessors have borne the results of nations', and vociferous mobs', manipulative directives, all designed to color the people's vision to unquestioningly accept what the elite powers (or loud self-proclaimed minorities) dictate. Although most politicos avoid references to Scripture, there is much to be gained by reading the historical record lying within those pages. Why? Because as much as everyone loves to quote, "those who do not read history are doomed to repeat it," they pay no attention to the wisdom of the statement.

Lamentations 2:9 – "Her gates are sunk into the ground; he hath destroyed and broken her bars: her king and her princes are among the Gentiles: **the law is no more; her prophets also find no vision from the LORD.**"

The foregoing was placed in boldface in order to bring attention to the so-called prophets of those times past that shed light on our modern day 'gurus.' In the annals of time, priests of the Temple were most often the ones blessed with the gift of prophecy, including Jeremiah, whose scribe, Baruch, documented all his prophetic visions, not once, but often twice as the princes of Judah destroyed the writings for fear of them and unwillingness to do what was necessary to avoid the consequences

(Jeremiah 32). Jeremiah, the author of the Book of Lamentations (where he wept and despaired over Jerusalem's ruin at the hand of Babylon's Nebuchadnezzar), tells us precisely what occurred. The kings, the noble progeny and powerful aristocracy had no interest in hearing what anointed prophets had to say (Isaiah 30:9-10 and, again, Jeremiah 32). They preferred to follow the uninspired preachings of 'prophets' that told them what they wanted to hear, that all would be well if they simply gave praise and glory to false idols, worship lies to ease their troubled souls and sanction their delusions.

The reason the 'visions' were uninspired "vain and foolish things," (Lamentations 2:4) is that "the law perish(ed) from the priests" (Ezekiel 7:26). The priesthood had served idolatry, subverting the truth for the sake of comfort and political correctness. Yes, even in ancient Judah and Israel was the PC concept a driving force. Read Solomon's Ecclesiastes to learn there is nothing new "under the sun," and all those purporting that collectivism is a new and bold concept haven't read history. This, of course, is the problem with our education system today. Just listen to students parroting their teachers who tell them that the study of history is irrelevant, the future is what counts.

To return to the point of this little exercise in historical analysis let's continue with the loss of the Temple priesthood's ability to prophesy truth. Their lack of connection to the most high (because of idolatry) left them bereft of receiving true knowledge from God to be shared with the chosen nations – Israel and Judah. They misled the people to believe lies, that what evil (idols) they followed were acceptable in the sight of God. Because of believing those lies, their profit turned to decay. They lost all to their foolish hunt after worldly riches, satiations and imaginings. Their families and goods were finally scattered and decimated after decades of refusing to hear the voices of the few genuine prophets of the time – among them Isaiah, who was martyred, and Jeremiah, who lived through attempts on his life to witness the fall of Jerusalem as it crumbled around him.

But who is it that suffered most? Lamentations 2:12: "They say to their mothers, Where is corn and wine? when they swooned as the wounded in the streets of the city, when their soul was poured out into their mothers' bosom."

The children ask for food and drink, the staples of life, only to faint with hunger and need amid the destruction wrought by their elders' foolishness, and the prophets' inability to see the true reason for their captivity, the languishing in servitude, banishment from their former life of plenty (Lamentations 2:14).

Lamentations 2:17 informs us that this loss had not come without warning. God told His people what would occur should they abandon Him for the worldly ways of the "gods" that promise fleshly fulfillment, (Leviticus 26:16) and now we repeat the cycle yet again. Our enemies rejoice over our loss, they consume our power (horn) to enhance their own (Lamentations 5:6).

But we are shown the way back to receive our inheritance – Lamentations 2:19: "Arise... pour out thine heart like water before the face of the Lord, lift up the hands toward Him for the life of thy children that faint for hunger in the top of every street." Thus, the hardship knows no bounds. All are affected by the evil we have done in turning away from our founding fathers' written covenant – the Constitution. Those who prosper at our demise are the enemy of the pact with Christian values (the basis of this document), with faith in God's plan and bounty. The usurpers of power (government officials, both elected and appointed) have been awarded, by our blindness and abdication of responsibility, the reins of control. This is the power of the penny through taxation, regulation and greed for more at others' expense rather than achieving for ourselves. (Lamentations 5:8: "Servants have ruled over us: there is none that doth deliver us out of their hand.")

Our downfall comes to looking for false gods (things of our creation upon which we bestow power) to "even the playing field" instead of working to do so ourselves by faith first, and secondly, the diligent labor to which God puts our hand.

We have looked for someone else to do it for us by making the sacrifice at the altar of foolishness and laxity, and have forfeited our rights by handing them to others meant to be our servants.

God has given us the answer. We must implement it… "Arise!... cry out… lift up our hands" and receive again the blessing He bestowed at the birth of this nation – true Freedom.

A. Dru Kristenev

✢ ✢ ✢

December 15, 2011
<u>Subverting language as a destabilizer</u>

In the days preceding the printing press and modern media, a clarion would sound the call for citizens to assemble in the village square, there to be apprised of important events by the town crier. This was the only real method of reaching the general populace in times past, which is why the phrase "blow the trumpet" comes up quite often in historical writings, including Scripture.

Jeremiah 6:1, 6:17, Jerusalem is instructed to attend to the trumpet (ram's horn or shofar) when it is blown to call the people to see the destruction on the horizon should they not turn from their wayward worship. The warning is given, God has placed watchmen to wind the trumpet, charging them with the duty of warning Israel (Isaiah 62:6; Jeremiah 6:17; Ezekiel 3: 17, 33:2, 6, 7, etc).

Their response to the alarm was this… "they said, We will not hear." Jeremiah 6:17. They refused to heed the call, soothing themselves with their own corrupt counsel. Where they are told to pay attention, take warning, the people's ears are closed, "behold, the word of the Lord is unto them a reproach (reminder of criticism, censure), they have no delight in it." (Jeremiah 6:10). Why they eschew the Word of God is plain, it doesn't condone the worldly works that feeds the flesh, leaving the spirit bereft and unfulfilled.

Yet the people appease themselves with their own advice, their "knowledge" – 6:14 – espousing "peace, peace: when there is no peace." The people give themselves over to covetousness (avarice) "and the prophet to the priest every one dealeth falsely." These are clear representations of how those in power spoke lies (Jeremiah 7:4, 7:8-9) and do so even in our times.

In some modern translations of the Bible we see a distortion of language that has augmented the collapsing faith of recent generations. Where in the King James Version the word is covetousness and unjust gain (Jeremiah 6:13, 8:10), in some recent translations (e.g. 2001 Literal Translation) the word has been changed to "profit," but the Hebrew word used, '*betsa*,' is clearly related to plunder, dishonest gain.

In fact, all but one usage of the term 'profit' in the KJV Old Testament is the Hebrew '*ya'al*,' which describes something valuable, beneficial, that does good. How does the word in the new translations drop to the very bottom of the barrel to define 'unjust gain' as 'profit;' i.e. '*ya'al*' as '*betsa*'?

Is it no wonder why students and fools crowd the streets, reaching the same conclusion that all profit is unjust? There's but one reason why some modern translations read it thus: their progressive public education which has twisted the idea of profit into something unclean, an act of personal aggrandizement that counters the law, the last commandment given to Moses – "Thou shalt not covet..." Yet by invoking this warped definition of the word 'profit,' what is it that the multitudes (okay, few thousands of OWS as opposed to the millions of tea partiers who understand profit) are advocating but that others' profit (valuable, beneficial earning) be given to the indolent who *covet* their property – all in direct violation of the Word and what is clear sense.

Profit is not a dirty word, covetousness is, and we are doomed to follow the lies of man if we do not heed that heralding call of the "watchmen" proclaiming the truth.

As Jeremiah said in 7:4, "trust ye not in the lying

words…" and 7:9, "will ye steal, murder and commit adultery and swear falsely…?" That is precisely what we, and our children, are being taught by the misdirection, misleading and misinformation of our NEA teachings. It is our duty to heed the call of the trumpet and read the Word, research our founding documents, laws and acts of Congress for ourselves. Not one of the politicians (also products of the progressive education agenda) has the whole answer. Many have all the wrong answers in attempting to make us believe there are bogeymen bankers and corporations forcing us to act against our hearts and wishes and the Word.

http://changingwind.org/index/comment.php?comment.news.112

The watchmen are responsible to blow the horn, but the rest of us are responsible to hear the call and listen.

A. Dru Kristenev

✠ ✠ ✠

Updated March 18, 2012…

With the re-emergence of the OWS movement at a St. Patty's day protest at NYC's Zuccotti Park, a couple of hundred people gathered vowing a spring offensive. http://www.foxnews.com/us/2012/03/18/occupy-wall-street-anniver-sary-ends-as-nyc-police-arrest-protesters/ *and* http://newyork.cbslo-cal.com/2012/03/18/ows-marks-sixth-month-anniversary-of-movement-with-demonstration-in-zuccotti-park/ *They were disbanded by police by midnight, some arrested for refusing to leave the private park that the Occupy crowd and their associates had, over six months before being removed last November by authorities, spoiled with crime, rape, drugs and unsani-tary waste. Must we brace ourselves for months more of the same degeneracy claiming democracy? If this is democracy in action, it should make us cry in gratitude for the republic that we have and must safeguard.*

OWS – The Fall of Jerusalem All Over Again

If you are not familiar with the events leading to the fall of Jerusalem in 70 A.D., all you really need do is review video of the various Occupy Wall Street confronta-tions to get a pretty clear picture of how it occurred (Oakland, NYC, Atlanta, etc.). First of all, for the purposes of this paper, it is understood that 70 A.D. was the "end of the age (aeon);" the end of the age of the Temple and ani-mal sacrifice; an end that came about in the most vile man-ner where atrocities were committed against innocents, neighbors and fellow believers.

This occurred at the close of the seven-year Jewish War. This is the war that was instigated against the institu-tion and rule of Rome, then the greatest power on earth, by people who believed that the prophecies of restoration of the Kingdom were to be fulfilled in their lifetime. They understood that Messiah's coming was imminent according to the timeline of the major prophets of the Old Testament, though they misunderstood the nature of His coming. In their fanaticism for throwing off the yoke of servitude, they rallied to leaders proclaiming a divine calling, including opportunists that glommed on to the rebel cause. These zealots and sicarii (terrorists and thieves) of which there were three factions, descended upon Jerusalem along with the multitudes of faithful come to honor the feast days, swelling the population to more than a million souls. What next occurred must give us pause.

The insurgents and zealots had lost skirmish after skirmish over the previous three and a half years of warring with Rome all across Judea, and they had slunk into Jerusalem under the guise of penitents coming to honor God during the Passover season. Once inside the walls, they battled with the other factions (also claiming to represent the true kingdom and reinstate freedom for the Jewish people) as well as the Roman legions occupying the city. Within a short period of time, the Romans abandoned the city to the unruly crowds raging through the streets murdering and robbing their own people.

The siege had begun.

As they fought amongst themselves to gain the upper hand within the beleaguered walls, which was overwhelmed by extra hundreds of thousands of individuals caught there during the feast days, the city was swamped with hunger, filth, lawlessness and unbelievable cruelty. Food, clean water, even housing was under a huge strain beneath the million people's survival needs.

The Temple, the most holy place on the earth, regarded worldwide as more beautiful than any other edifice built to

honor man or God, was targeted by the zealots, who, in the name of freedom, camped out in the courtyard. The Temple was utterly trashed, demolished and overrun with sewage and rubbish by the party that had claimed it as their headquarters from where they were convinced they could wrest freedom from Rome. Murder came quickly on its heels, ***Works of Flavius Josephus,*** War of the Jews, Book 5, Chapter 1. (For an eyewitness account of the demise of Jerusalem read this for yourself and see the correlation of what is occurring under our noses in all our major cities. Josephus' chronicling of the Jewish War is alarming and a salient warning.
http://www.biblestudytools.com/history/flavius-josephus/war-of-the-jews/)

Reprise the fall.

If this doesn't smack of the unruly mobs we've witnessed prowling the streets of New York, Portland, Oakland and Washington, D.C. then you must be sitting in a blacked-out, sound-proofed box.

In January there was a particular report of a citizen (one of many) in Washington, D.C. who was surrounded and threatened by the rabble at McPherson Park because he had the gall to hope to enjoy the public park as it had been created – a pretty, peaceful green space in the midst of the cityscape. The angry crowd had usurped the public space for their personal place to express their vendetta against, what? Frankly, I haven't heard a single explanation from an OWS spokesperson that has made any sense as to their purpose. In any case, in their expression of anger at whatever it is (if you know the answer, give me a call) they hemmed in this individual and assaulted him with epithets and expletives, telling him that they had a right to seize that public place and ejected him from their "camp." http://www.foxnews.com/on-air/america-live/index.html#/v/1427881706001/retired-police-officer-mobbed-by-occupy-group/?playlist_id=87651

This is the ugly face of foolish, misguided and destructive anger at the world in general; the undermining of civilized interaction, only to be replaced by lashing out like animals with expectations of receiving civil response from authorities in return. Do they really expect to be treated respectfully by the very establishment for which they have afforded none? This is so by the playbook instituted by John of Giscala, Simon the Zealot and Eleazar during Jerusalem's devolving into ignominy, setting the once lovely streets alight with fire and to run with blood. It doesn't take much imagination to see our own temples of government (since it has replaced God) going up in flames and the lawless hedonism dancing in the public ways.

The OWS gangs are generously sponsored by those progressives (mostly George Soros) who would happily view the downfall of capitalism and all it has built (even their own vast fortunes, as what was good for them must become off-limits to others, entrenching their powerbase), favoring the bedlam that leaves the door wide open for them to waltz in with their own form of deliverance – one that benefits the one (themselves) and not the many, allowing themselves power and OPM. For, isn't this exactly what the OWS cries to attain? Equitable redistribution of someone else's wealth? This is precisely what the zealots and sicarii did to Jerusalem, that holy golden city, stripped it bare to feed off the fat in their wantonness, only to lose it all as Rome bided its time outside the walls, awaiting the collapse from within. Titus stood by patiently waiting to swoop in and gather the spoils, all the warring factions dying from infighting.

Understand that the complete demise of civilized intercourse in favor of chaos that helps no one is the exact opposite of what Christ came to usher in, true freedom. Freedom is found in throwing off the slavery of the flesh, what the Law addresses, in favor of the spiritual completion of ourselves through grace. The Temple's destruction and end of the age, "not one stone shall be left here upon another…" (Matthew 24), as in complete demolition of the foundation in favor of another foundation to be laid, was fulfilled by the blood sacrifice of Christ laying that new foundation that no other imperfect physical sacrifice be needed ever again (Hebrews 10:12-14). The flesh (power-seeking) brought about the destruction of the age of blood sacrifice for redemption, and was replaced with the spiritual instruction of freedom by serving one another through caring for one another, not tearing apart each other for gain, *other people's* earnings. In this context the Temple = imperfect physical satisfaction: strife; Christ = complete spiritual fulfillment: peace.

To raze the place where you live through actions of brutality and betrayal, thinking to create a better life, is worse than folly. To idly sit by and watch the demise occur, assuming that everything will even out, is criminal. Power comes through the freedom of Christ's peace, understanding that no real satisfaction can be found within the fleshly existence. The material world and any attempt to physically "occupy" a thing or place brings nothing but more contention, contempt, unhappiness and deplorable behavior. Is this where this great country is headed? A repeat of pain, bloodletting and sorrow?

A. Dru Kristenev

✠ ✠ ✠

March 3, 2012
Court of Law – Temple Court

The concept of a "court of law" can be directly related to the temple court where the Pharisees convened and the Sanhedrin (judicial council) presided in Jerusalem. Here they judged according to the Law, the commandments of God, the ten written by God's own finger we are familiar with as the prevailing guidelines for a sanctified life and the 613 or 603 statutes, depending on the Talmud teacher's understanding – which are symbolized by the number of thread windings of the tzitzit (tassels) on the tallit (prayer shawl).

According to Scripture, the Pharisees were judgmental regarding the application of the law, and were often referred to as "lawyers," even unto this day.

Merriam Webster definition of phar·i·see:
1. *capitalized* : a member of a Jewish sect of the intertestamental period noted for strict observance of rites and ceremonies of the written law and for insistence on the validity of their own oral traditions concerning the law
2. a pharisaical person
Origin of PHARISEE
Middle English pharise, from Old English farise, from Late Latin pharisaeus, from Greek pharisaios, from Aramaic perishayya, plural of perisha, literally, separated
First Known Use: before 12th century
http://www.jewishencyclopedia.com/articles/13178-sanhedrin

The temple court was where Jesus taught the crowd and was challenged by the legal faction…

Luke 20:1 "One day as Jesus was teaching the people in the temple courts and proclaiming the good news, the chief priests and the teachers of the law, together with the elders, came up to him. ² "Tell us by what authority you are doing these things," they said. "Who gave you this authority?""

The pertinent word in this Scripture is authority. The priests, elders and scribes approved each other's authority in the law, reading it, interpreting it and applying it to other's actions, often while overlooking their own falling short of it – sin.

Quick to cast stones, as is seen when the Pharisees were preparing to pass sentence on an adulteress for her transgressions, Jesus called them out on that very principle. When Jesus confronted them with their own inadequacy in keeping the Law, Matthew 8, they relented. The temple court was the place of judgment, where teachers and strict followers of the law convened to apply the Law according to their own discernment.

It was here in the temple court that Jesus threw over the tables of the merchants. At exorbitant prices, they were selling doves to be offered as sacrifices, the cost so high that the offering was beyond the ability of many to buy. Do we see why He called it a "den of thieves?" Justice with God was attained through the sacrifice for sins, the sin offering of the unblemished animal or fowl. The concept was carried forward in the church during Medieval times when priests gave absolution for sins to those who purchased it, thus making the process one of commerce rather than repentance to receive redemption. Think how the correlation to legal proceedings today is yet apparent in that justice was more than the poor could pay, much as we see now... legal representation is often out of their financial reach.

Although the phrase "court of law" may also be derived from the King's court where the sovereign passed judgment on questions of law (of which the monarch was the ultimate lawmaker and arbiter), still it can be traced back to the judgment of God. From the time of the Ark's housing in the tabernacle, God judged those who approached the sanctuary through the court that stood before it by their station. Numbers 3:38, "Moses and Aaron and his sons were to camp to the east of the tabernacle, toward the sunrise, in front of the tent of meeting. They were responsible for the care of the sanctuary on behalf of the Israelites. Anyone else who approached the sanctuary was to be put to death."

The modern invocation of a "court of law," man's appointed judiciary and officials of the "court," has taken over the role from God and his Word, which gives us our commandments for living well with one another. The lawyers and judges, having usurped this power, now hinder the path to justification, sanctification and atonement for wrongs we incur against God's principles. The statutes of man have now become the bellwether of right and wrong replacing God's commandments:

Mark 12:30, "Love the Lord your God with all your heart and with all your soul and with all your mind and with all your strength.' 31 The second is this: 'Love your neighbor as yourself.' There is no commandment greater than these.'" And the road to redemption is no longer paved with change of heart but with monetary offerings to the "court," its officials and the legislators who create the laws and read them – today's Pharisees.

A. Dru Kristenev

✤ ✤ ✤

April 23, 2012
<u>Complacency: Murder of Nations</u>

What this campaign cycle is proving thus far is that party politics is beating down those who would see an active renewal of our Constitutional Republic in favor of the status quo, i.e. more of the same indolence and self-indulgent, self-serving expectancy that someone else will do what's needed.

Deny it all you will, but it is complacent acceptance of what is, assuming that if we do nothing, nothing will change. Yet we have been promised change, and as history testifies, change of this sort is to our detriment.

Much as most people these days like to say that studying history is a waste of time as being irrelevant to the present and most certainly the future (I cannot tell you how many times I've heard that, not only from my students but from my professorial colleagues), I am compelled to take us back to look at the history of nations collapsing, no, *being murdered* by the inertia of complacency.

What is meant here by complacency is the rationalization of: 1) Assumption of powerlessness; 2) Allowing pressures of personal provision to overtake our lives to the utter exclusion of all else; 3) Abdicating responsibility of governance to that of others.

This is how we placate our conscience to carry on as usual, heads buried in the sand, dum-de-dum, and as the late newscaster John Chancellor described the influence brokers' operating standard during the 1968 Democrat Convention: "sie-de-die, la-de-da, and boop-boop-be-doop."

Now to the history lesson, lest I lose your interest if I

haven't already…

The cultures and vast empires that have disintegrated under the populace's ambivalence are numerous going back millennia: Israel and Judah, Babylon, Athens, Judea, Rome, Nazi Germany, USSR; the list is actually unending. As most national entities suffer demise after reaching an apex of economic dynamism, the reason isn't hard to understand. What is most difficult to swallow is to what depths of depravity many of them sank on the way down. No matter who ruled, it was the egocentrism of the powerful and their overly indulgent lifestyles that allowed the middle management to usurp control. Those who styled themselves as "defenders of the poor" (now termed "disenfranchised"), the ones who arrive on a (tarnished) white horse, stating their intentions of giving a hand up that is always a hand*out* of someone else's wealth.

Examples of the downward spiral of nations include Israel and Judah as the people left their roots of working toward common liberty under God's law, to tolerating and finally instituting the practices of pagan nations that manifested as going-along to getting-along even to the point of human sacrifice. (No, I'm not going to load this up with links because most won't bother to check anyway – they'd rather just refute without researching.) Is this any different from what the Nazis brought to the easily swayed German people, so frightened of falling deeper into economic collapse that they acceded to debasement of their culture and, in effect, human sacrifice for the "good of the whole?" AKA the Holocaust.

Not to be forgotten are all of the in-between nations that deteriorated through infighting – Alexander's empire that disintegrated into the Seleucid, Ptolmaic Empires, etc., which themselves were overrun by Rome; the Goths that waltzed in Rome's front door, sacking it while the idle hierarchy ignored the borders over time, Byzantium still holding its own in the East only to be overtaken by the rise of Mohammed's caliphate. The tales go on and on as to how the ruling class strove for power, more and more in a vacuum, until an incursion of outsiders, or uprising of envious packs of indigenous poor provoked by the "intelligentsia," overtook governmental control, usually with even less compassion for their compatriots than the previous despots. Just look to the French Revolution and Robespierre (who was a lawyer, by the way), and the butcher Ché Guevara (a doctor who managed the central bank for Castro) among the numerous examples.

Brief as is this overview of human history, is the picture gelling? When those who hold power, be it through a dynasty, republic or democracy (there is a distinction between the last two), lose focus of their purpose, giving in to the blindness of self-centered existence, then the fabric of society unravels. Moths eat at the threads as forces of Nature tear the tapestry from top to bottom, all while the people scramble to find a morsel to eat, sometimes stealing from another to do so. This is how nations dissolve… all in favor of tunnel vision into a mirror's reflection of "me."

This complacency is precisely what has brought us to the current brink of loss, of liberty denied and an amped-up goose-step, rolling over the ambling oblivious attitude that most of Americans hide behind. Keep it up. Tell us that politics is boring, evil, arrogant and/or purposeless and, so, you have no interest. Or you already have too much on your plate to give the running of your country any attention. It's easier to be non-judgmental and uninvolved.

This is the formula for murdering a nation… our nation – denying our responsibility. Just like it's our responsibility to feed ourselves and our families, if we do not stand up for what's right and what's hard (as opposed to what's convenient) there will no longer be an option of properly laying a table. Someone else will have hoarded what's left while the rest of us starve, and not just for a meal but, more importantly, for freedom lost.

My point in all this? Don't settle for the party line, or the so-called heir apparent. Take a stand to be certain that you have a voice come decision time. Right now we have two of the same vying to institute more of the same (Obama and Romney), and it's hard to fathom why the vast chorus of voices would allow this to be the final choice. Depends on how concerned we really are about the future, but this choice is no choice. There is one still standing who knows American history *and* his way around a federal budget (and how to get it passed) that the media is purposefully ignoring... Newt.

Send a message to party leadership that it's not their role to foist a candidate upon us, but for the voters to do the choosing.

A. Dru Kristenev

✛ ✛ ✛

July 13, 2012
Let's go back to Egypt; Freedom is just too hard

If you've been wondering how this Supreme Court of the United States came up with the ruling on Obamacare, we have an answer that most will not only dislike, but totally disavow. You may want to read this anyway.

It's all about me, and "me" is indolent. This is the first and foremost premise that underlies the whole situation with which we are now saddled, meaning the stripping away of freedoms right and left by every "representative" and judicial referee (as the court is little more than this) of the People. Assuming that the Constitution is now nothing more than a parchment with unenforceable scribblings, each of the branches of the federal government has taken upon itself to mandate (isn't that a popular word) what American life will consist of, dictating what your life will be in the years to come. And, evidently, we are so consumed by living our lives that we prefer to acquiesce to those "mandates."

A point we'd like to make: these "mandates" only stand as such if we accept what our so-called *representa - tive government* has accepted, that the average citizen is indeed too preoccupied (busy with self-centered activity, otherwise known as chasing one's tail) to take notice or care enough to implement the Constitution as it was written: as the parameters of a government formed by a series of mandates of the people upon such government, limiting its purpose and power to serve the People, not itself. This is the true meaning of "Liberty."

Having said this, let's move on to exactly how every one of us has been bamboozled by the "*federales*." To begin with, we have decided to loosen language to the point where we no longer understand the written word of the Framers instead of reading the Constitution in the context with which it was penned, being fully apprised that each clause of an article of the Constitution is affected by the previous clause. The clauses do not stand alone without context. (See Federalist Papers Number 67 through 70 for a series of illustrated examples of this very same *sepa - ration misrepresentation* of the Constitution used by the anti-Federalists.)

Article VI, Clause 2 exemplifies this. For some reason we have been led to believe that treaties supersede our own Constitution due to the misreading of the clauses because we no longer understand grammar. Read this section as, "This Constitution, *and the Laws of the United States that shall be made in pursuance thereof*, …, shall be the supreme Law of the Land;"… The other sentence portions relate back to the Constitution and all Laws… **made in the pursuance thereof"** as being what holds the highest authority, not treaties and certainly not laws that are passed through Congress **unconstitutionally.** Read it for yourself, please. If you haven't a copy of the Constitution, go online and download one, or read it here at the National Archives, http://www.archives.gov/. If the whole Congress, the President and the Supreme Court call it Constitutional, yet it clearly did not pass muster as having been emplaced according to Constitutional standards (see http://changingwind.org/index/comment.php?comment.news.121 for an explanation of the law and rules of process necessary for legitimate passage of a tax that were bypassed in the instance of Obamacare), then a "law" is not enforceable, nor is a treaty if it abrogates the limits we placed on government to assure absolute protection of our unalienable rights, or any clause of the Constitution whatsoever. And there is no confusion here, for this same self-executing clause of the Constitution that renders acts of Congress without any supremacy works identically upon treaties, for that is its purpose by its construction.

Problem is, how indolent are we, how removed from our founders' legacy have we become that we'll turn back time and happily trip down the road back to Egypt, the known servitude, and thus easier life, because we then need not make decisions for ourselves, simply go along for the ride, however bumpy, and settle for relinquishing the freedom we once enjoyed?

Yes, that's a mouthful, but how true is it when the NAACP is willing to look the return of slavery in the face, and applaud its ugly countenance, (no offense Mr. Biden) then turn around and jeer a candidate that offers a return to self-sufficiency, self-reliance, exactly what the organization is supposed to embrace? It is nothing more than a travesty when any one of us Americans is willing to resign ourselves to receive a meager handout, one that undercuts the hard work most of us, irrespective of our color, creed or ethnic origin, have labored to enjoy... all in order to accept a government *acquiescence stipend* as reward. It is giving up and returning to Pharaoh's rule because the trek has a few hills that must be climbed.

And the incline in question is turning the tables on the governing bodies that have deduced that the People will allow the Constitution to be sidelined in exactly the way we have witnessed with this last SCOTUS ruling on Obamacare. The ruling of the mandate being a tax and all 193 pages (which I read and took copious and, come to find, irrelevant notes) should be roundfiled – the ashcan, for those of you who have gone paperless and don't recall outdated lingo – as superfluous for the simple reason that the so-called tax, and all 18 or so taxes within the "law" was not passed according to the supreme Law of the Land, the Constitution. Toddy wrote on this extensively: Healthcare Process & Legality— An Indictment Of Progressives In Government, Son of Single Payer, More Evidence Healthcare Law Unconstitutional, Unconscionable Is Unconstitutional, and this is just the tip of the iceberg.

So the question is posed, "how do we enforce the Constitution and rein in the government, which is clearly operating outside of constitutional bounds?" The solution lies within the articles above and it hardly makes sense for us to reiterate, yet again, what is plainly written therein.

The real question is, if you are still reading this, "are we so weak and poor of spirit that we will not put up a "fight" to relegate government back to its true place, as servants of the people, and not as a means to establish a political ruling class?" In all truth, I'm not so certain we have the chutzpah to do it. I hear the groaning of the people who grew tired of manna. We have become inured to the stripping away of rights, little by little and bemoan our loss of a government handout, the Pharaoh's largesse.

So, what'll it be? Laboring for Pharaoh to gain a little grain and a pat on the head, or head out for the Promised Land. The milk and honey ahead is actually behind us if only we would see where God placed us with the grace of His mercy and Thomas Jefferson's attendance to God's Word **in writing the lines and those following, that read:**
"IN CONGRESS, July 4, 1776.
The unanimous Declaration of the thirteen united States of America..."
This means what it says according to Noah Webster's 1828 American Dictionary, "In Congress,"
n. [L., to come together; to go or step; a step. See Grade and Degree.]
1. A meeting of individuals; an assembly of envoys, com -

missioners, deputies, &c., particularly a meeting of the representatives of several courts, to concert measures for their common good, or to adjust their mutual concerns.??
2. The assembly of delegates of the several British Colonies in America, which united to resist the claims of Great Britain in 1774, and which declared the colonies independent.

The Constitution came from this authority of Congress, not the reading of justices in a court created by and after Congress. Congress has the capacity, if we use our power to instate individuals willing and ready to enforce the Constitution, to write and repeal legislation that **must adhere** to the true Law of the Land, not afterthought statutes. In fact the Judiciary Act of 1789 created a multi-justice U.S. Supreme Court and the judicial system as we know it, which is a rather powerful statement of how Congress is sole source from which Government derives. This is self-government by representation, better known as a Republic.

Now, can we get the order straight?

Thank you for reading,
A. Dru Kristenev with Toddy Littman contributing

✛ ✛ ✛

September 22, 2012
<u>Trampling our landmarks</u>

One of the most common questions parents and teachers hear is, *why study history when it has no relevance to my life?* It's becoming a refrain that has insinuated itself into every aspect of our lives. Everything we do, see and experience is about the future, relegating the past to, well, the past.

If you are one who believes that looking ahead is the best, most positive approach to life, that the motto of *Forward!* Is all we need to succeed, allow me to make my case… again.

Realizing that many are not students of Scripture, considering it to be an exercise in futility to read what is thought to be a compilation of fairy tales that have no bearing on our lives today, let me make this point before you discontinue reading. When compared and correlated to secular historians and archeological finds throughout the last four to five millennia, much of it has been corroborated as accurate chronicling of occurrences in the Middle East.

That said, permit me to expand on our lesson from the past; actually lessons, plural.

Over and over again, the stories of the Israelites explain the consequences of foolish and self-centered behavior. Throughout the first five books, revered by Judaism, Christianity and Islam all, the example of disregarding the high road, or plain sense, to follow one of self-aggrandizement and pleasure-seeking hounded these more than a million souls roving through the desert wasteland. As you've heard before, an 11-day journey took 40 years because they continually lost sight of the big picture: that of serving a higher purpose than themselves. For those of us who believe, I'm talking about God.

Now that I have probably lost more of my audience, let me continue. The Pentateuch was only the beginning of the 'tangled web we weave,' if you'll pardon the borrowed phrase. Moving through every book of the Old and New Testament we have exactly what it says, testaments to man's imprudence, the unnecessary throwing away of sensible choices in favor of personal 'fun.' This isn't to say that one should not enjoy themselves, what these historical books do is detail how fulfillment is better found in loving, patient and purposeful thoughts and acts than the temporal (and injudicious) gratification.

For this is where the egoistic lives led, not just once, but repeatedly, to social collapse.

Jerusalem, which stands as an archetype of every society that has taken the egocentric path, was treated to multiple devastations over centuries. The continual overrunning of Israel in the time of the Judges approximately every 40 years (each generation that forgot the lessons of their parents); the destruction of Jerusalem around 580 B.C.; the city's debasing by the Seleucid and Roman empires; and ultimately the final destruction of the city in 70 A.D. that wiped out over a million people through plagues of famine, fire, bloodletting, drought and siege. A pretty miserable testament, wouldn't you agree?

There is an alternative future outcome that can be learned from this record when we look back to Scripture and see the parallel of what Jeremiah witnessed in the Babylonian conquest and what our nation is experiencing today. Lamentations 5 states what he *actually* saw, had warned would come, and what, if we remove our blinders, we shall see today.

With this statement I assume further attrition of readership. That's to be expected, no one wants to confront awkward facts if it forces self-examination of our part in any of it. And believe me, we have all played a role.

If you'll stick with this a little longer, I will add a few quotes that you can apply for yourself if any of this has made sense to you. Lamentations 5 (ESV):

"[1]Remember, O Lord, what has befallen us; look, and see our disgrace! [2]Our inheritance has been turned over to strangers, our homes to foreigners. [3]We have become orphans, fatherless; our mothers are like widows. [4]We must pay for the water we drink; the wood we get must be bought. [5]Our pursuers are at our necks; we are weary; we are given no rest. [6]We have given the hand to Egypt, and to Assyria, to get bread enough…"

It behooves us to read the full chapter if we can stomach it.

An answer looms clearly that we can follow well if we will only relinquish our clutch on what we *feel* about what's right and embrace what we *know* is right. America has an incredible source of wisdom that laid the foundation for its existence, the written Constitution that has been dragged through the mud by unrepentant editors that have rewritten it in their own image of right, an image of emotion rather than reason. We have a duty to hear what Solomon had to say on the subject in Proverbs 22:28 (KJV) – "Remove not the ancient landmark, which thy fathers have set."

For those who would quibble over the meaning of that landmark, turn back to the other monuments they left for us to apply to gain inarguable understanding of it: the Declaration of Independence, which states how America was born; and the Federalist Papers, which the brilliant minds of Alexander Hamilton, James Madison and John Jay penned before the Constitution was ratified so we would ALL have their intent at our fingertips, fully explained for our edification.

Why we do not avail ourselves of both the lessons of the past and the template for the future is to our disgrace. Next time we fervently yell *"Forward!"* be compelled to read from whence we have come, *then* make a reasoned, rather than an emotional, decision on how we should proceed as a nation.

A. Dru Kristenev

✙ ✙ ✙

November 6, 2012
<u>Tears for fools</u>

For many years we have prayed and worked to restore understanding among the people of what this nation is truly, its beginning and its hope for a bright future, but few have listened.

In this presidential election cycle, as I watched the continued demise of America, succumbing yet further to following the faithless paths that have been laid by faithless leaders (Proverbs 6:16-19[i]), I could do no more than prostrate myself in prayer and cry for our nation, our subverting by idolatry that has led to this pass of destructive behavior; the craven want for what others possess driving half of the populace to accept iniquitous conduct and pull the whole nation down in their wake.

As the tears flowed, I was reminded of David's realization of his own transgression, the stealing of what little another goodman had, his wife. Knowingly had he sent the man to his death in order to obtain the prize, but when the prophet Nathan told him a parable to bring home David's wrongdoing, the king repented. 2 Samuel 12.[ii] The son he fathered by the wife he had stolen became ill and David fell on his face to plead for the child's life, as I was pleading for the life of this nation, but judgment had been passed… the child died just as this nation is now in the throes of its dissolution.

It is time to dry my eyes and set aside the weeping. As David said when they wondered at his grieving no longer once the babe had died, "Can I bring him back?" it is not for me to continue to mourn what is past because, anymore than David could revive his son, we cannot revive the nation with tears, only with striving to do what is right despite the mass of dupes who despise God and the gift He gave us of America.

Benjamin Franklin warned us that we would lose this Republic if we were not vigilant enough to keep it safe, and we have allowed ourselves to be wooed by envy of worldly goods, believing ourselves deserving of riches we did not create, to take (redistribute) another's wealth as our own.

I've cried enough. It will not reinstate the greatness that was America. Though I will continue to pray for mercy upon this nation and our return to wisdom, I will not waste my tears on fools.

A. Dru Kristenev

---

[i]**Proverbs 6:16** There are six things that the Lord hates, seven that are an abomination to him: 17 haughty eyes, a lying tongue, and hands that shed innocent blood,
18 a heart that devises wicked plans, feet that make haste to run to evil,
19 a false witness who breathes out lies, and one who sows discord among brothers. (ESV)

[ii] **2 Samuel 12** - And the Lord sent Nathan to David. He came to him and said to him, "There were two men in a certain city, the one rich and the other poor.
2 The rich man had very many flocks and herds,
3 but the poor man had nothing but one little ewe lamb, which he had bought. And he brought it up, and it grew up with him and with his children. It used to eat of his morsel and drink from his cup and lie in his arms, and it was like a daughter to him.
4 Now there came a traveler to the rich man, and he was unwilling to take one of his own flock or herd to prepare for the guest who had come to him, but he took the poor man's lamb and prepared it for the man who had come to him."
5 Then David's anger was greatly kindled against the man, and he said to Nathan, "As the Lord lives, the man who has done this deserves to die,
6 and he shall restore the lamb fourfold, because he did this thing, and because he had no pity."

7 Nathan said to David, "You are the man! Thus says the Lord, the God of Israel, 'I anointed you king over Israel, and I delivered you out of the hand of Saul.

8 And I gave you your master's house and your master's wives into your arms and gave you the house of Israel and of Judah. And if this were too little, I would add to you as much more.

9 Why have you despised the word of the Lord, to do what is evil in his sight? You have struck down Uriah the Hittite with the sword and have taken his wife to be your wife and have killed him with the sword of the Ammonites.

10 Now therefore the sword shall never depart from your house, because you have despised me and have taken the wife of Uriah the Hittite to be your wife.'

11 Thus says the Lord, 'Behold, I will raise up evil against you out of your own house. And I will take your wives before your eyes and give them to your neighbor, and he shall lie with your wives in the sight of this sun.

12 For you did it secretly, but I will do this thing before all Israel and before the sun.'"

13 David said to Nathan, "I have sinned against the Lord." And Nathan said to David, "The Lord also has put away your sin; you shall not die.

14 Nevertheless, because by this deed you have utterly scorned the Lord, the child who is born to you shall die."

15 Then Nathan went to his house. And the Lord afflicted the child that Uriah's wife bore to David, and he became sick.

16 David therefore sought God on behalf of the child. And David fasted and went in and lay all night on the ground.

17 And the elders of his house stood beside him, to raise him from the ground, but he would not, nor did he eat food with them.

18 On the seventh day the child died. And the servants of David were afraid to tell him that the child was dead, for they said, "Behold, while the child was yet alive, we spoke to him, and he did not listen to us. How then can we say to him the child is dead? He may do himself some harm."

19 But when David saw that his servants were whispering together, David understood that the child was dead. And David said to his servants, "Is the child dead?" They said, "He is dead."

20 Then David arose from the earth and washed and anointed himself and changed his clothes. And he went into the house of the Lord and worshiped. He then went to his own house. And when he asked, they set food before him, and he ate.

21 Then his servants said to him, "What is this thing that you have done? You fasted and wept for the child while he was alive; but when the child died, you arose and ate food."

22 He said, "While the child was still alive, I fasted and wept, for I said, 'Who knows whether the Lord will be gracious to me, that the child may live?'

23 But now he is dead. Why should I fast? Can I bring him back again? I shall

go to him, but he will not return to me." (ESV)

✠ ✠ ✠

Part 3

Foreign Policy

June 9, 2009
Casting pearls before swine

The president's insistence on traveling to Muslim countries in order to pay homage to his religious "roots," (though some might argue that he never left them) while practically disowning the heritage of his own nation, brought this maxim to mind.

Know that this likely will be the most obnoxious and offensive comparison made to the Palestinian debacle as seen by Muslim adherents. However, at every turn when the Palestinian contingent has been offered a concession it has been utterly rejected in favor of waiting for their hopes of Israel's impending doom to be fulfilled.

Albeit the homily – "…neither cast ye your pearls before swine lest they trample them under their feet. And turn again and rend you…" – was offered by Jesus to those who would hear his ministry, when taken beyond the spiritual context, it is plain common sense that Israel and America should heed.

What the Palestinian leadership has done to its own people over the last 60 years is what Obama is now attempting to do to America in a matter of months. Is it extreme to even float this concept? Perhaps, but let me state my reasoning.

The Palestinians were offered citizenship within the new state of Israel upon its inception in 1948. Instead of sharing in the democracy being constructed, they were incited to flee the meager borders of the new Jewish state, fired by a fear that was fanned by their own mullahs and neighboring Arab nations.

As the decades marched on and despite the Israelis rebuffing every effort by the hateful actions of Palestinian leadership and surrounding Arab nations to crush the young country, compromises were made on the part of the victors. The Sinai Peninsula was returned to Egypt after the Six Day War of 1967 and later the West Bank and Gaza were delivered back to Palestinian control. The Golan Heights is an anomalous region of contention in regard to the other territories.

Since taking control of the West Bank, the Palestinian Authority has attempted to make a few improvements for their constituents. Yet in most cases, wherever Palestinians have been given land with developed infrastructure, solid housing and other amenities (note Gaza under Hamas' control), the first step of the new owners was to burn the "tainted" goods handed back, install bases to continually bombard their Jewish neighbor, and demand yet more of the land/wealth until the producer, Israel, should be destroyed. Trampled pearls indeed.

Over the last decades protestations against industrious and successful Americans, who have created wealth while others wallowed in self-induced poverty, have greatly increased. Not all who suffer disadvantages have placed themselves in that position, but most who see themselves as the underclass have been whipped into believing that they are victims of the wealthy – which definition has steadily been trimmed back to include the moderate income earners. With the election of our current president, the ferocious demolition of the economy of America has been underway. At every turn, President Obama has called for the dismantling of the financial and manufacturing industry in order to parse out the wealth to the clamoring "leadership" of contrived victims.

Yes, in both situations there are people suffering. The reason for their suffering can be traced back to misguided leadership that feeds people misinformation and rhetoric that keeps them in the dark and living the life of less when they could be pursuing more. Israel has placed its citizens in jeopardy by attempting to placate the hatemongering of Palestinians, Arab hardliners and Islamic terrorists. America's hard-working producers have been backed into a corner by the despicable acts of rabble-rousers that incite the less fortunate to call for the producers' demise while Congress hands over one concession after another. In each case, there will be no pacifying the angry mob until the demonized producer is ruined.

As odious as it sounds, casting pearls before swine (in other words, giving to the ungrateful, or telling truth to the deaf) does not implicate the followers so much as the exploitive leadership that compels them to reject the extended open hand in favor of a raised fist. Under their expert tutelage, the only answer by Palestinians to parley (and American "victims" to want) are resentful demands for the contributor/producer to be laid bare and banished from what they have built.

The pearls of wisdom are not only trampled but they are lost to all.

A. Dru Kristenev

✤ ✤ ✤

June 7, 2010
<u>Who Do We Save First?</u>

We have been called to duty more times than we can
count, as individuals, as communities and as a nation. It is
our identity as Americans, stemming from our Christian
roots (no matter how much the Left protests the fact of the
matter) that drives us to do what is right, to protect the
innocent and feed, clothe and house the poor. How many
of our ancestors came to these shores in want, hoping
beyond hope that a new beginning awaited them? The
shining light of America beckoned them to leave the
poverty and escape the shackles of tyranny that reigned in
the foreign lands of their nativity. My own grandparents
were among those seeking refuge from the pogroms of
Russia.

The catchword here is "nativity." For, once they had
set foot in this land, crossing the seas or borders, petitioned for admission to this country and eventually settled
down, they acquired a form of nativity, a re-birth, through
the process of naturalization, the mutual adoption of nation
and citizen.

Re-birth. Birth. The framers of this country had it
right, you know, when they came together to sign the
Declaration of Independence. Freedom and equality begin
at birth, and in this 'Land of Liberty' that is when we
pledge our loyalty to this nation, whether we travail as
individuals for the privilege of citizenship, or if our parents' travailed to bring us into the New World and achieve
citizenship. Equality is bestowed upon us at birth, from
thence onward, equality, in every sense, is what we make
of it. It is not bestowed by government, nor is it "redistrib-

uted" by said entity according to wishes or needs. It is something for which we must work and succeed. Freedom is the warp and weave of America's fabric, which means we are free to make the most of the equality, that the founding fathers asserted, through our own efforts.

What this also means is that we have undertaken the calling to be a beacon of freedom and equality as a light, a signal fire, to the rest of the world. If that sounds arrogant, it is not. It accepts the profound trials over which our forefathers triumphed, in the name of invoking our unalienable rights "endowed by their Creator."

Let me clarify, when the writers of this document referred to the Creator, they were not referring to any government, king or despot, or indeed, any man or manmade institution. They were acknowledging God as the architect of all things. Hence, by accepting that all men are created equal in the sight of their Creator, we, as Americans, are duty-bound to share that vision with others by example. We have been known to be the most charitable nation on the earth, and, lest we forget, "charity" is the all-encompassing love of God, the Creator who endowed us with this freedom in the first place. As such a nation given to giving, it has become an expectation of other countries, feeling the need and want moreso than we, that we share our bounty. Indeed we have done so and will continue to do so as time wears on, yet there is now a caveat.

By what means will we continue to offer material salvation to the poorer countries if we no longer have the largesse to share? And this is not a rhetorical, disingenuous statement. This is based on clear fact that the distorted view of our nation's beginnings and ultimate purpose, as colored by the current administration's policies, are voiding the capacity and industriousness of our people, negating our ability to give to others.

What is the answer then, if we are to continue to save others from the ravages of worldly greed and sinister business practices? If our resources are so vacated that we have nothing more to dole out to the rest, the more needy, then there is nothing left but universal poverty and a few multi-national thugs lording it over the masses, wallowing in the wealth they've stolen from the hard-working.

The answer is plain. We must first save ourselves. The collapse of economies under the ever-growing burden of massive government bureaucracies, entitlement programs and corruption and mismanagement will strike our shores if we do not "shore-up" our bastions. They have already been pouring across our southern border. We are the only nation capable of weathering the coming storm **because** of the groundwork laid by our founders, because they supplied us with the recourse to withstand abusive government policies and spending.

No other country on earth has the framework that do we in order to correct our course, for, "When in the Course of human events it becomes necessary for one people to dissolve the political bands which have connected them with another and to assume among the powers of the earth, the separate and equal station to which the Laws of Nature and of Nature's God entitle them, a decent respect to the opinions of mankind requires that they should declare the causes which impel them to the separation..." we are compelled to steer back to harbor and begin the voyage again, reclaiming these words and instituting them properly.

Let us take up the task, run the rigging, swab the deck, clean the hull of barnacles, reset sail, and chart a new course based on the trusty compass points we received from our nation's framers. We must save ourselves from the approaching tempest and find anchorage before we can offer safe harbor to others.

A. Dru Kristenev

October 12, 2010
<u>Since when is religion a race?</u>

The latest uproar by Arab citizens of Israel over a bill requiring new citizens to take an oath of allegiance to the 'Jewish and Democratic' state is yet another misdirection of word use, and it is the press that's causing the stir.

Nowhere within the quotes from Arab leaders, that I could find, has the term "racist" appeared. Yet the mainstream press is crying that the Arab minority within Israel is labeling the new amendment to a bill, that was passed by the Cabinet by a vote of 22 to eight on Sunday, October 10, 2010, as being so.

Yes, the Arab leadership was claiming that the legislation would undermine their rights within the nation. However, despite the AP asserting (without providing any facts to back the contention) http://tbo.ly/bBqXQT that the Arab minority suffers general discrimination, this is one population that is provided equal rights under Israeli law and is well represented within the legislative body. Today's miniscule protest, staged at Tel Aviv's Independence Hall, of 150 foolhardy artists and academics, who live in a world of their own contrivance, claimed Israel is now 'fascist' for taking a stand on it's right to exist as a nonexclusive homeland for Jewish people. The smattering of rabble-rousers was unworthy of international press coverage, proving yet again how far the media will go to create controversy.

http://www.jpost.com/VideoArticles/Article.aspx?id=190913

Prime Minister Benjamin Netanyahu clarified the rationale for the bill as being necessary to remind the world that the State of Israel was established to be a home-

land for the dispossessed Jewish people
http://www.jpost.com/Israel/Article.aspx?id=190831. People who
truly had been discriminated against, to the point of
attempted extermination not sixty years ago by an actual
fascist nation.

How quickly the world forgets.

They forget also that the slow migration of Jews, back
to what was historically considered their homeland, took
place over decades of immigrants purchasing square miles
of empty tracts from the absentee Ottoman Turk landlords.
No one really lived there aside from nomadic Arabs who
were not called Palestinians, in that there was no Palestine.
The term was instituted at a later date when the whole area
came under the purview of the British Empire, which utilized the Roman name to describe the region. This area of
the Middle East was essentially underpopulated to the
point of being virtually barren. Even the land itself was little more than desert, with some malaria-infested swamp,
that was revitalized by displaced Jews from Europe who
developed the first drip irrigation systems.

And calling Israel racist? This isn't the first time the
epithet has been thrown at the Jewish state. In fact, I wrote
a paper on this very issue when the United Nations first
levied the charge, branding Zionism as racist in 1976 with
a resolution that was unwarranted and utterly fatuous.
Neither Zionism nor Judaism are racist, or can be
described as such. Zionism is a political philosophy, and
Judaism is a religion. Racism is generally related to cate-
gorizing humans by skin color, and even here the term is
misapplied more often than not.

Over and over again, people misuse the word 'racist'
by employing it to describe ethnicity, a completely different standard. Whether one is Hispanic, Arabic, French,
Azerbaijani or Polynesian, these titles indicate ethnicity in

regard to one's native culture and language. It has nothing to do with race. In fact, the idea of race is consistently misapplied assuming that it is a categorization of people by skin tone, which it is not. The concept of races (of which there are only three – Caucasoid, Mongoloid and Negroid) was originally assigned according to the geographic origin of a people (e.g. Australian Aborigines are classified as Caucasoid, as are Polynesians).

I hope that this is computing with all of you who constantly abuse the terminology in order to instigate divisiveness. Yes, that's what I said… diversity is based on division of people, not the opposite, and all hypocrites who insist upon stressing the differences between people, particularly here in the United States of America, are nothing better than provocateurs.

Media must be responsible for the words they use and headlines they blare, seeking only to create rifts and undermine communities and nations. It belongs to us, the people, however, to correct misuse of language and ignore the destabilizing media and the agitators who would only degrade our society for their own gain.

Recognizing the reason why a nation came into being and pledging allegiance thereto, is no premise for division, but one of cohesion, wherein all citizens of that nation share equal rights under those laws. Israel is a democracy, different in its establishment from our own republic, but the people must uphold the state to which they profess loyalty as citizens. Look to the Pakistani immigrant who was just landed behind bars with a life sentence for attempting to destroy citizens of his adopted country, the USA.

An oath of allegiance must have meaning for a naturalized citizen of any nation, let alone a bitterly embattled state such as Israel.

A. Dru Kristenev

Scripture Led Politics

✥ ✥ ✥

Part 4

Thoughts on the Holidays

December 23, 2009

It Came Upon a Midnight Clear...

Actually, it was about 3 a.m. but the skies were crystal and cold. What am I talking about? A Christmas message for me that seemed significant enough to share, and it clarified some correlations between Scripture and how we mind the business of our lives and our neighbor's lives.

It started for me with the realization that it has been 40 years since the first Christmas after the death of my mother. This triggered some thought about the 40 years the Israelites wandered in the wilderness, opening a door in my mind that maybe I've inadvertently followed in their footsteps. Not a pleasant thought, but as this year has unfolded, I've begun to realize that my penchant to cling to past experiences has kept me in my own personal wilderness for the span of a generation.

All right, this may sound like idle musings about why the Israelites meandered the desert, however these ponderings brought me to understand that I have perpetuated their same fault. Doubt.

Early on, the Lord led and protected the Israelites through every avenue of escape from slavery. He gave them a beacon to follow, opened the seas and fed them every day in their sojourn. The story of the manna alone is the lesson that most struck me. God gave them daily sustenance that could not be stored. They needed to collect the gift of the day's provision every morning. If they attempted to hoard more than was necessary for their nourishment, it would be gone. The Israelites were being given a daily message that they can, should and must trust the Lord in **all** things. Doubt would be their undoing, yet they did not understand or accept His gift in the manner it was meant.

Instead, they couldn't even contain themselves for the 40 days it took Moses to receive the written Law from God and deliver it to them. They doubted. They crafted an idol and cavorted in its presence, placing faith in something of their own making and not the wonderment of God's proven gifts. They paid the price… 40 years of waste, leaving the Promised Land to the next generation.

There are many correlations here, in my estimation. To doubt God and His ability to supply all you need is manifested in the action of hoarding. As much as the Lord tried to teach the recalcitrant Israelites that hoarding (doubt) is futile, they still murmured and complained that what He gave wasn't enough. They wanted more and paid the price. My own price is intensely personal, but it is a price all the same, and the overall lesson that I received is what I'd like to share.

Christmas Eve all those years ago, we didn't want to spend the night at home. It had been a very special time for my mother and we were all too raw to even attempt to approach the holiday with cheer – and here I use the scriptural sense of the word, 'courage.' We packed up the car and went to the drive-in to watch the new release, "Scrooge" with Albert Finney, which is still one of my favorite Christmas films. But it was only this last "midnight clear" as I pondered the 40 years, that brought home yet another meaning of hoarding.

Yes, hoarding is the embodiment of doubt, but it is also the physical and spiritual storage of waste. All kinds of waste. Hoarding riches is wasteful because it is never used to anyone's benefit. Not the hoarder, not the poor. It piles up in one's heart as well as in one's household or bank account. But why do we hoard anything? Because we doubt God's ability to adequately provide for us.

I am not disparaging prudent saving, hoarding goes far beyond that. It is waste stored in one's body, perhaps as pain or fat or even, if you'll pardon my being crass, constipation. Scripture associates the bowels with the core of our very being in numerous instances, both physically and spiritually. In fact, Christianity is not the only faith or philosophy that does so.

Waste is a stumbling block for many of us because we will continue to doubt and rely on the instinct to hoard, giving in to the animal part of our construction rather than the spiritual which the Lord placed in our hearts. Scrooge had help to figure it out and we do too if we give ourselves over to the Lord to complete the equation.

But that takes faith.

Faith is something that has become lacking in our society and the runaway Congress is proof of that. Many have abandoned the faithful founding of this nation that was cobbled together by men of faith who studied the Word and were guided down the path of freedom.

Doubt is now the way of life. We so doubt our purpose that we have given over to hoarding. Oh no, we aren't compiling the riches personally, we've given that onerous duty to government to do it for us. Let the Congress tax and hoard and what do they do? They create legislation that is filled with literal and actual waste. TARP, Stimulus, and the federal budget alone are monstrosities of compiling waste that is not getting to the hands of the needy, it is filling the coffers of the rich – those that feed off the vulnerability of the poor as did Scrooge, the privileged members of Congress and financial bottom-feeders – not the productive business builders who provide employment for the would-be poor.

If this has been too rambling for you, let me break it down into my little epiphany. To doubt is to hoard; to hoard is to amass waste; and waste is what a miser compiles that is beneficial to no one… the hoarder or the needy. And accumulating waste poisons the body, be it an individual's or the body politic.

For me, it's been 40 years and I, like the new generation of Israelites, am ready to accept God's gift of Faith.

As we celebrate the birth of Christ, our Savior, may God bless you in your journey,

A. Dru Kristenev
With special thanks to Toddy Littman and his tremendous insight.

✛ ✛ ✛

September 10, 2011
<u>What cost liberty ten years after 9/11?</u>

Recalling the first assault against our country to occur on the continent since the War of 1812, can overwhelm most of us when we picture where we were upon hearing the news, or watching the collapse of the twin towers in full color.

Shock. We reeled with it. Working a health ministry in rural Idaho on that fateful day, without television, radio was our only access to immediate news. And we were listening to talk radio when the reports came flooding in about a plane crashing into the World Trade Center in New York. We were aghast at the bulletin, wondering if it could be a replay of an Orson Wells-style hype. It wasn't long before the news broke of a second plane careening into the sister building and the rapid implosion that followed. But the day was not done for these practitioners of evil. The Pentagon was afire, and, in Shanksville, Pennsylvania, heroes plummeted to their deaths in the course of waylaying their jet's hijackers hell-bent on blazing their way to paradise via Washington, D.C.

The knowledge that heinous deeds had been perpetrated against our country, the world's bastion of freedom, was almost beyond our comprehension. Not in almost 200 years had the continental United States suffered an invasive attack by a hostile enemy. But to what of our existence were these immoral adversaries antagonistic?

Liberty.

This is a concept completely and utterly inconceivable to those who exist under a tyrannous creed, a dogma that curtails all free thought and activity. Thus, they irrationally perceive our way of life to be a threat to theirs. Whether that autocratic doctrine is religious or political, it all comes to the misconception that, without repressive rules to guide every step one makes, life is not worth the breath it takes to fill one's lungs. This is the mentality, the insecure, self-doubting attitude that drives people to embrace intransigent beliefs. To waver from one's deeply-rooted conviction that has been thrust into a mind for all their waking hours, be it in the classroom, home, or place of worship (including governmental institutions) is unimaginable. In actuality, a theocracy could be anything from an Islamic state to a communist, as both require an unquestioning faith in the system, and its leaders. What it truly entails is the total relinquishment of individual thought, purpose and fulfillment. In other words, this country, the freedom envisioned by our Founding Fathers, is simply anathema to the Muslim group-think, and, by their reckoning, only fit for destruction because they cannot understand its premise.

The proof of our liberty is the fact that we can discern between free thought and that which is circumscribed to impose "order," otherwise known as despotism, the purpose of which is to control, plain and simple. The only people (religious or political) who require control are those who wish to retain wealth and power unto themselves, a closed society that our founders had already tasted, and knowingly fought against to acknowledge the sovereignty of God, who is our one and only definitive ruler.

So we remember the cost of freedom: the willingness to be hated, and to stand opposed to brutality no matter what evil may be wrought against us. Because freedom is the ability to express oneself by word, faith and calling; to create wealth for oneself and family, and to share that prosperity as they see fit, blessing others with largesse without regulation or direction by governmental bodies, religious or bureaucratic.

It is a steep price to pay, but it is one that we recognize and readily give, when others prefer to be extorted of their God-bestowed right of freedom by power-hungry autocrats and self-proclaimed rulers.

A brief memory of 9-11-2001 by Toddy

Living in California at the time, I was, at best, a moderate who was leaning Liberal. People all around me against George Bush, explaining how Gore was robbed, while also telling me they didn't want to pay taxes, yet complaining about not receiving some entitlement check on time, and always ready to blame the Federal Reserve for every problem America has. I was a believer in the notion we did this to ourselves, someone who believed this deluded notion so strongly, I denied myself the sadness, denied myself the life that comes from truly experiencing the grief of the moment if I had been thinking of others. But, instead, there was anger at Bush and the idea that government had done this to us on purpose, as a way to declare martial law and brand us with the mark of the beast. The year 2000 computer glitch was supposed to make that happen, but failed, and of course, that created an excuse to think the next event would be the final one, that they weren't prepared to take over and control us when 2000 came.

The above are the thoughts I deluded myself with, until, I ran across an effort to make an internal impeller of the jet that struck the Pentagon, an object they were claiming means it was a small plane, to lie about what really happened, just to say George Bush and the U.S. Government did this on purpose, as a hoax, as a reason to go to war. It was the research to prove the government was behind 911 that began a review of all of what I believed, and helped me understand just how much of what I knew was merely propaganda to feed my desire to believe in wrong more than right, a desire to distrust more than find the truth and appreciate reason. As I discovered how wrong I was then, by details and facts that could only be seen once I set aside the bias that blinds, I found my way back to the traditional, to the comprehension of America, of Freedom and Individual Liberty, to learn the irrationality of trying to legislate order from a chaos that Liberty naturally manifests in the difference between each of us, that yet, due to Liberty, becomes our similarity, what makes us Americans.

So, today the memory of the nearly 3,000 Americans who lost their lives to terrorism brings home what true terror is: living without Liberty.

A. Dru Kristenev and Toddy Littman

✛ ✛ ✛

November 24, 2011
Thanksgiving when we most need to believe...

This year many are facing wholly unexpected circumstances, situations that were beyond their imagining a year or two ago. It may be family dispersed, finances dissolved, households in disarray... the stable times being replaced by insecurity, perhaps even loss.

These are times, no matter where we find ourselves, be it at the head of the table in the family dining room or surrounded by others queued up to receive the blessing of a meal at a charity kitchen, when we must recall what has been taken for granted throughout most of our lives. It may be, by Providence, that I am in a position by which to order these things in my mind and my heart.

For more than a year, I have had the opportunity to travel this country in ministry. Not the kind of mission work that is sustained by a particular church or denomination, being unaffiliated with institutions; but having a ministry that is simple... that of sharing the Word of God, our Christ Jesus, through the few gifts He has put in my charge. It has been an eye-opening experience to take the leap of leaving a well-ordered life, travel this nation and be invited into homes to share their bounty, or lack, as the case may be.

The core of our country is comprised of generous people, who often give when they can least afford to do so, those who understand the nature of our beginnings and our sovereignty. When we recall the words spoken by President George Washington as he answered the call for a national day to give thanks to our true provider, God, he did not forget the years of struggle, hardship and loss he and his neighbors had suffered in order to create this exceptional nation...

"Whereas both Houses of Congress have, by their joint committee, requested me "to recommend to the people of the United States a Day Of Public Thanksgiving and Prayer, to be observed by acknowledging with grateful hearts the many and signal favors of Almighty God, especially by affording them an opportunity peaceably to establish a form of government for their safety and happiness:

"Now Therefore, I do recommend and assign Thursday, the Twenty-Sixth Day of November next, to be devoted by the people of these States to the service of that great and glorious Being who is the beneficent author of all the good that was, that is, or that will be; that we may then all unite in rendering unto Him our sincere and humble thanks for His kind care and protection of the people of this country previous to their becoming a nation; for the signal and manifold mercies and the favorable interpositions of His providence in the course and conclusion of the late war; for the great degree of tranquility, union, and plenty which we have since enjoyed;– for the peaceable and rational manner in which we have been enabled to establish Constitutions of government for our safety and happiness, and particularly the national one now lately instituted;– for the civil and religious liberty with which we are blessed, and the means we have of acquiring and diffusing useful knowledge;– and, in general, for all the great and various favours which He has been pleased to confer upon us."

Any words that I may write cannot come close to expressing the fervor of our first president in acknowledging God and His role in what we now benefit: a free country, should we choose to keep it.

Consider the last words written above. We have made

foolish choices in keeping our own counsel rather than that of God, decisions that have placed us upon a threshold of once again losing the liberty for which these men and women fought so diligently. Instead of giving thanks where it is due, we have raised up generations that expect to never experience hardship or want, they demand what they do not understand, rising up in the streets proclaiming disenfranchisement when they are so incredibly endowed with plenty that they cannot recognize it.

Being challenged to travel this country, taking nothing but the Bible as guide, and faith as provider, has expanded my perspective further than I could have anticipated, to recognize the power of hope and standing strong in the face of adversity. History teaches us that when we relinquish our connection to God, our Creator, and follow our own thoughts, giving praise and worship to false powers created by man (Jeremiah 44:15-20 – you might like to insert "government" in place of Queen of Heaven), then do we lose our baseline, direction and, ultimately, our liberty. Desolation occurs in the heart first and the land follows.

President Washington spoke the words by which we can live and give thanks with clear conscience, knowing that whatever circumstance or wherever we find ourselves on any day, not just Thanksgiving Day, we realize that from which this nation arose... from servitude to man, a king, to freedom in God's bounty. Remember at what cost was our liberty won and give praise and thanks to our Creator, to Christ, who led our forefathers, through faith, to establish what we now take for granted.

Wherever you may be, under shelter or a chandelier, Thanksgiving Day is a reminder of the hope, faith and sacrifice made for each of us.

God bless,
A. Dru Kristenev

✙ ✙ ✙

December 20, 2011 – Study for Christmas
<u>Freedom Parable... Zechariah 8</u>

Jealousy, that is the word God used to describe His protectiveness of Zion, and the fury that He felt at Israel's betrayal by following false gods (Zechariah 8:2). Still did He tell the prophet that He returned to Zion, "and dwell in the midst of Jerusalem: and Jerusalem shall be called the city of truth..."

In that day, approximately 520 years before the birth of Christ which we celebrate this day, God promised that the aged and the young will again become denizens of Jerusalem, the city that had been destroyed and emptied of inhabitants at the hands of the Chaldeans (Zechariah 8:3). Children will play, running up and down the streets (Zechariah 8:4). The Lord says He will turn the adversity of the past to prosperity and joy in the future (Zechariah 8:10-13). He will alter Israel and Judah from being "a curse among the heathen... ye shall be a blessing: fear not, but let your hands be strong."

This is also the story of the remnant of Israel, the Lord reopening the land to His chosen, a thing "marvelous in the eyes of the remnant..." (Zechariah 8:6-7) as He says that He "will save My people from the east country and from the west country." In other translations, "the land of the rising sun and the land of the setting sun," but the tale is the same, God would, and did, bring together the captivity to dwell in Zion.

But the story is also a parable... the literal Israelites never did return to Jerusalem. The ten tribes dispersed to Assyria – Ezekiel 5:10, "and the whole remnant of thee will I scatter unto all the winds" – before the southern kingdom, Judah, went into captivity. Although Judah returned to rebuild the temple (Ezra 1:2) Israel became wanderers among the nations (gentiles), assimilating into the pagan societies. "And the LORD said, Even thus shall the children of Israel eat their defiled bread among the Gentiles, whither I will drive them." (Ezekiel 4:13; see Ezekiel 5:2 and 12, Jeremiah 23:8, Isaiah 11:12, 43:5-6).

Yet God told Zechariah that they will find blessing and He gives them (and us) the means by which to receive it. Zechariah 8:16, "These are the things that ye shall do; Speak ye every man the truth to his neighbour; execute the judgment of truth and peace in your gates:"

8:17, "And let none of you imagine evil in your hearts against his neighbour; and love no false oath: for all these are things that I hate, saith the LORD."

Of course, it's quite evident that so many within these borders of America are not practicing the directive not to conceive evil against their neighbors (such as the Occupy crowd chanting that the rich are the enemy, spouting class warfare), not to give one's heart to swear falsely by the name of God (Matthew 5:33). This comes as insincerity, false oaths taking the name of God in vain, which is to swear falsely by His name, particularly <u>calling oneself a believer when **one believes not** in Christ as savior.</u>

Many people of the world (nations, gentiles) shall seek the Lord in Jerusalem (Ezekiel 8:20-22). Is this not a parable to the seeking of Freedom, called forth by the Lord, in the lands of America?

This, a prophecy of Christ and the ten tribes that would re-emerge from the nations (Israel as the assimilated gentiles) to believe on the Son and His Sacrifice: Ezekiel 8:23, "In those days it shall come to pass, that ten men shall take hold out of all languages of the nations, even shall take hold of the skirt of him that is a Jew, saying, We will go with you: for we have heard that God is with you." It is also a shadow of the nations spilling their people from over their borders to make the passage to a new land, be planted with new hope, grasping the robe of the Savior and the freedom He embodies that formed the root of a new nation unlike any other before seen on earth.

Christ is the catalyst for bringing the gentiles into the fold, as well as the embodiment of true Freedom established by "the protection of Divine Providence" upon which our founding fathers relied as they declared independence, pledging their Lives, Fortunes and sacred Honor.

The circle is complete in seeing the dispersion of Israel gathered at the foot of Christ, accepting the Creator's freedom by returning the seekers of liberty (the faithful) to the shores (His skirts) of this nation.

Be blessed in your sojourn of freedom this Christmas Day!

A. Dru Kristenev and Toddy Littman

✤ ✤ ✤

September 11, 2012
From Vibrancy to Fatalism

It had been 22 years between my visits to New York when I arrived there in the fall of 2010. I had come to town for multiple reasons: to visit with my longtime friend, a resident of that great metropolis since the 70s; to assist with a ministry; and to gather up-to-date background for my forthcoming book, ***Blood Barons***.

The effervescence that had pulsed up and down the arterials stretching the length and breadth of Manhattan in 1988 was noticeably absent this time around. The weather was beautiful for October… sunshine, soft breezes and the trees in Central Park just beginning to take on that hint of fall color. Strolling through the streets, enjoying a break at a sidewalk café here and there, I was able to compare the snippets of idle conversation that drifted past to what I had heard years past. The tone had changed dramatically.

I'm not certain if New Yorkers realize any difference that time and one particular event has done to alter the energy pervading their city, but it was palpable to me, an outsider. Years earlier, a snowfall had swamped the streets just before we'd flown into town. It was still awash with vitality as people rushed about their business, avoiding the mounds of snow piled by the corners. We spent the few days catching up with friends and family, taking in a couple of Broadway shows and doing the usual tourist thing.

This time, the air of expectancy and dynamism was missing. The friendly banter overheard told more about stress-laden lives, employment woes, relationship strains and, well, melancholy. One of the women in our ministry group had grown up in the city and I put the question plainly, "What happened?"

"Nine eleven," was her answer. She told me how that day had virtually changed the underlying temperament. There had been a shock of violation as the dust from the twin towers' collapse permeated the air. She did tell me how people quickly relied more on each other for support and bucked up to do what needed to be done. Jumping back into the fray as the economy came back to life with a roar, people worked with a renewed drive, but in many ways, New York, and the rest of the country, still hadn't recovered to that previous level of vitality.

The installation of a new administration in the White House had brought a brief flicker of hope that was snuffed with a breath of wind, as the economy continued its nose-dive. When I arrived in 2010, a sense of resignation lingered. The aftereffects of 9/11 left a mark of vulnerability that had yet to be erased.

The people of this great city had bonded after that brutal attack and those following attempts by sick individuals to recreate the horror, hoping to beat them into submission, only strengthened their core. But it has been tempered by the fatalism of the current administration constantly telling us that, not only could no one have brought us out of the economic slump, but we are stuck with it and the steady outpouring of wealth in a failed attempt to prolong the decline. With leadership like this, no wonder the New York malaise was so tangible to me and those with me.

The tale of 9/11 is one of camaraderie in hard times. It is not an acceptance of mediocrity, which is what the President has been pushing us, the citizens of this nation and especially the survivors of tragedy in New York, D.C. and Pennsylvania, the heroes of the day, to tolerate.

We can take hold of the faith and *true* hope that these, our neighbors, embodied, and throw off the pessimism that is preached from the Oval Office. There is too much at stake to allow a mindset of demise and frailty to be the legacy of 9/11. We are stronger and more confident than that, just as the populace of NYC was buoyant in going about their daily business in 1988. What's changed? The people haven't. The vision, or lack thereof, of America by our government has.

May we recall the courage that was demonstrated both on that day and each one following, taking heart that this nation, under God, is blessed as we institute real change and not transformation Obama-style.

A. Dru Kristenev

✣ ✣ ✣

Scripture Led Politics

Epilogue
Salt of the Earth

Matthew 5:13 - "Ye are the salt of the earth..."

Most Christians have some understanding of that to which Jesus was referring when he called his disciples the "salt of the earth." For me, some years back the concept led me to examine my purpose and ultimate journey. Having spent nearly two decades studying, praying and laboring to reach others about our nation's course, of which readers may or may not agree, this was a conundrum that called me to study how I am meant to fulfill that identity of the salt. And not myself alone, but how our Founding Fathers met this portrayal of faith and how millions of us today can do the same.

It calls for a willingness to look beyond ourselves in terms of need and desire, a capacity that has diminished significantly over the decades, may I say even over the last century. The Greatest Generation pulled us back from the chasm of self-indulgence and victimhood but, as it seems, only temporarily before we again began blazing down that path at an ever-increasing speed.

To be the "salt of the earth" we must focus on how our actions affect others including our nation as a whole. This requires taking a stand on what is right rather than allowing wrongheadedness, however well intentioned it may appear, to push us over the brink into the darkness of spiritual and literal poverty.

Perhaps we should consider why Jesus used this metaphor...

Salt (sodium chloride) is unique as a mineral. It is a naturally occurring part of the earth itself, as man was created from the clay (mineral) of the earth. It is not an herb, fruit, leaf or bark of a tree, or vegetable which the earth supports, growing it up from seed. Salt is unlike any other mineral in that it is used as a seasoning, enhancement and preservative. It is also unlike any other seasoning in that it is a naturally occurring mineral whereas herbal seasonings must be cultivated, collected and dried. Thus saffron, oregano, cinnamon or even pepper does not have a similar origin or the qualities of salt.

Salt has an effect, either hot or cold, on everything. Salt on the snow (thrown out and trodden under the foot of man) melts the snow, perhaps keeping some capacity to yet melt the hard heart of man even as it is tossed out, as Christ was crucified outside the walls – Hebrews 13: "12 Wherefore Jesus also, that he might sanctify the people with his own blood, suffered without the gate. 13 Let us go forth therefore unto him without the camp, bearing his reproach."

How does salt correspond to our role as believers?

The salt of the earth is the enhanced man.

The salt is the seasoning that releases the flavor, the spiritual nature of man. It's the ingredient that preserves and enhances flesh, thus preserving man, the soul, from spoilage or ruin, which would naturally occur if he follows his own mind – Proverbs 3: "7 Be not wise in thine own eyes: fear the Lord, and depart from evil."

Salt is the catalyst (Christ) that brings forth the essence of man, completing in spirit what is otherwise simple flesh, the catalyst that enhances man. Without salt, flesh will rot, as without the preserving agent, Christ, man will decay.

How do we as the 'salt of the earth' perform our duty to Christ?

The saints, the faithful, the spiritually awakened within Christ (those who are the salt) are the preservation of man, steering him from destruction, becoming guides to others to also find purpose. Purpose within God, believing, serving one another and so serving God (Matthew 25:37-40[i]).

Being the salt (sharing the Word, Christ) brings thirst. As such, the salt, we may lead others to drink the Water of Life (John 4:14[ii], Revelation 21:6[iii]) that the thirst for more knowledge of Christ be quenched in knowing him and studying God's Word.

The foreshadow and fulfillment of Christ...

Leviticus 2:13 - "And every oblation of thy meat offering shalt thou season with salt; neither shalt thou suffer the salt of the covenant of thy God to be lacking from thy meat offering: with all thine offerings thou shalt offer salt."

Blood is salty and it is Christ's blood that washes us clean of sin. (Revelation 1:5[iv]) His blood was spilled for us, as the sacrifices presaged, yet the salt that was offered with those sacrifices also foretold the salt that spiritually enhances our lives through the Word; and the final blood sacrifice made once for all. (Hebrews 10:10[v])

Colossians 4:6 – "Let your speech be always with grace, seasoned with salt, that ye may know how ye ought to answer every man."

Again, the salt is the truth of Christ and the grace, the mercy freely given us by His sacrifice on the cross that blesses each of us when we speak it and share it.

Losing the saltiness...

"...But if the salt loses its saltiness, how can it be made salty again? It is no longer good for anything, except to be thrown out and trampled underfoot." (Matthew 5:13)

Mark 9:49-50 – "For everyone will be seasoned with fire, and every sacrifice will be seasoned with salt. Salt is good, but if the salt loses its flavor, how will you season it? Have salt in yourselves, and have peace with one another."

As one person noted[vi] who made a goodly point that I just happened across, they observed how salt loses its savor, its inherent saltiness when it is diluted in water. "...it would have to be diluted in water because it is non-reactive in its crystalline form. Or electricity would have to be introduce[d] to force the sodium chloride into its ionic components thereby changing its chemical composition [and being salt no longer]." They went on to describe the one who had lost saltiness. "This person is the complacent Christian," the one for whom the Gospel, the Good News is diluted in their life, becoming lukewarm (Revelation 3:16[vii]), diluting the Word with other philosophies, making espoused faith vain by contradiction and the "salt" good for nothing.

The point that is made is the point that Christ made, that we, as disciples, are exhorted to be steadfast in learning, applying and witnessing the truth. This means that it must be a part of our every action, thought and breath. Yes, we will make mistakes, but if we are diligent in studying and sharing the Word, we are also forgiven and allowed a new start based on the "once for all" offering of Christ's sacrifice for us, grace. It is for us, then, to be conscientious in every aspect of our lives, seeing that what we are constantly being taught through the Word is part and parcel to how we live, including the institutions of justice and legislation, which rely on political assertion of ground rules stemming from God's Good Word.

In all, faith and politics cannot be surgically severed and are not mutually exclusive, for without faith (the guidelines of forgiveness and justice) political action will have no purpose or even effect on society. We are motivated to apply faith in achieving a society of moral and equitable (not "even" by means of redistribution, but by equal prospects to achieve and give) roots. This is the liberty and justice fulfilled by Christ and how we are the "salt" to season and preserve this nation, touching this world and enhancing it, just as our Founders did.

So, how do you interpret salt? And how will you apply that definition to season your life and that of others?

God bless!
A. Dru Kristenev
ChangingWind Ministry

---

[i] **Matthew 25:37-40 (KJV)**

37 Then shall the righteous answer him, saying, Lord, when saw we thee an hungred, and fed thee? or thirsty, and gave thee drink?
38 When saw we thee a stranger, and took thee in? or naked, and clothed thee?
39 Or when saw we thee sick, or in prison, and came unto thee?
40 And the King shall answer and say unto them, Verily I say unto you, Inasmuch as ye have done it unto one of the least of these my brethren, ye have done it unto me.

[ii] **John 4:14 (KJV)**

14 But whosoever drinketh of the water that I shall give him shall never thirst; but the water that I shall give him shall be in him a well of water springing up into everlasting life.

iii Revelation 21:6 (KJV)

6 And he said unto me, It is done. I am Alpha and Omega, the beginning and the end. I will give unto him that is athirst of the fountain of the water of life freely.

iv Revelation 1:5-6 (KJV)

5 And from Jesus Christ, who is the faithful witness, and the first begotten of the dead, and the prince of the kings of the earth. Unto him that loved us, and washed us from our sins in his own blood,

v Hebrews 10:10 (KJV)

10 By the which will we are sanctified through the offering of the body of Jesus Christ once for all.

vi http://deneenwhite.com/2007/01/06/how-does-salt-lose-its-saltiness/

vii Revelation 3:16 (KJV)

16 So then because thou art lukewarm, and neither cold nor hot, I will spue thee out of my mouth.

✥ ✥ ✥

www.ingramcontent.com/pod-product-compliance
Lightning Source LLC
Chambersburg PA
CBHW070105070426
42448CB00038B/1728